Inner Child Healing

How to Recognize Childhood Trauma and Heal Your Inner Child by Reparenting Yourself

Milena Harrett

Table of Contents

Trigger Warning

The topics discussed in this book revolve around mental health conditions and past trauma. If you find the concepts outlined in this book triggering and you have difficulty facing past experiences on your own, please note that you do not have to go through the healing process by yourself. Psychotherapy is an effective way to deal with past trauma. With the help of a psychologist, you can identify your trauma triggers and find ways to overcome them.

When I first started practicing the concepts we'll discuss in this book, I sought out professional help. Talking to a therapist positively impacted my healing process.

Introduction

Beautify your inner dialogue. Beautify your inner world with love, light, and compassion. Life will be beautiful –Amit Ray

Inside all of us is a child who longs to be loved, seen, heard, protected, and acknowledged. From childhood, we have developed certain behaviors—some good, others quite harmful to our well-being as a means to cope with past pain.

I know how it is to feel empty and confused about your life and be unable to find the answers to the questions that plague you. I also know what it is like to fear intimate relationships because you do not want to get too attached to the other person, the need for people to please just to find validation, and the struggle to find your identity in this already complex world we live in.

I have experienced how suppressed emotions can affect your entire life—your self-image, how you interact in your relationships, your beliefs, and your life choices.

If you are at that point in your life where you are tired of emotional pain and are looking for a way to find peace, calm, and healing, I wrote this book with you in mind. Not so long ago, I was where you are—struggling with an eating disorder and body dissatisfaction. I worked hard to change my body image. I practiced journaling and positive affirmations every day. However, during this process, I realized that all this work that was cited and recommended to be effective in any healing process was not as effective as I thought it would be. It was certainly not the magic formula that would eventually cause the negative beliefs I had about my body to dissipate. I found out that I had deep-rooted body-image issues that were way bigger than I thought and that they needed to be resolved. For some time, I wondered where these issues were coming from.

You see, healing can be messy, which is why most people are afraid to do the necessary work to heal their past trauma. Sometimes life can feel like you are floating on top of an iceberg in the middle of this vast ocean. You cannot help but wonder how deep the iceberg goes beneath the surface. It takes courage to dive deep into the vast ocean of your emotions to find out where your feelings, fears, frustrations, and impulsive behaviors stem from and how they impact your life.

Taking a step toward self-healing is a sign of courage, and I commend you for your determination to overcome the emotional struggles you are facing. Not everyone is brave enough to face their dark emotional side. Most people end up living half a life because they allow fear to cripple them, and their past experiences dictate how they live their lives.

The thing about holding onto emotional pain is that it consumes you slowly and gradually turns into either uncontrollable rage, frustration, or anxiety, which eventually turns into depression. Most people suffer in silence—afraid of being judged—and therefore, instead of sharing how they feel, they suppress their emotions and find escape and temporary relief from food, television, alcohol, drugs, sex, and other external stimuli to help them cope.

The Effects of Past Trauma

We all have our personal experiences—from our childhood to our adulthood. Some of these experiences were pleasant, and others... not so pleasant, which left most of us emotionally scarred. Our childhood experiences shaped who we are today and our entire worldview. They shaped our belief systems and influenced our behaviors and how we interact with the world around us.

If you have started out on your healing journey, you may have noticed some uncomfortable feelings and emotions that come up from time to time. You might even wonder where these feelings are coming from and why they surface at specific moments.
Growing up, you encountered different people in your life—from caregivers to school teachers, friends, and neighbors. All these people played a role in developing your self-concept, your view of relationships, and your outlook on life in general. From these childhood experiences, you developed your identity and coping mechanisms to help you adapt to the environment you grew up in.

We may have had different experiences growing up. Whether you grew up in a dysfunctional family with caregivers who were emotionally unavailable or you were bullied and made fun of by your peers in school because of your physical appearance. The results of these traumatic childhood experiences are the same. They interrupted your normal, healthy neurological and psychological development as a child.

To survive these traumatic experiences, most of us had to hide our true essence underneath the deepest, unconscious parts of our human psyche. What emerged was a false self that has been running our lives and detecting the way we behave.

The problem with this false self is that it is not entirely you. It is partly the sum of all the coping mechanisms you learned from your childhood until now to help you survive.
When you become aware of this truth, you realize that you have been living your life trying to control the outcomes of your life and wanting to be right in order to gain a sense of self.

Identifying Your True Self

The first time I heard about inner child healing was when I was recovering from an eating disorder. After all the work I had put into trying to change my body image, I soon realized that the way I felt about my body was not going to change and I needed a different approach. For me to gain an understanding of where my body image issues came from, I had to go back into my childhood and find out the reasons why I was dissatisfied with the way I looked. I discovered some deeply-rooted and painful experiences I had gone through growing up that were influencing the way I felt about myself.

Through inner child healing, I managed to accelerate the process of working on and improving my emotional issues.

Although inner child healing helped me overcome my eating disorder, I did not realize at the time how powerful the concept was in healing other aspects of my life. After recovering from my eating disorder, I stopped practicing the concept for a while.

Healing is a process. Recovering from past trauma and painful experiences takes time, patience, and persistence. Sometimes we become impatient and want immediate relief from emotional pain. We just want to get to the finish line and skip all the work that needs to be done in between—before we win the victory. It was after I got into my first relationship and things turned ugly that I decided to practice inner child healing once again. The first year of my relationship went by without any complications. It was blissful and passionate, like any other new relationship. As time went by, my partner and I got into serious arguments. It would start with a small issue, and we would completely blow things out of proportion. The arguments eventually became frequent and often left us both feeling extremely overwhelmed.

We were totally flabbergasted at what was happening to us. At this point in our relationship, I was so overwhelmed and needed a way to find healing. I began searching the internet for answers and remembered that I had once read about someone who healed her relationship through inner child healing. Because I was already familiar with the concept, I decided to practice it again, even though I thought I had healed all my wounds after overcoming my eating disorder. Little did I know that I still had so many wounds that needed healing.

I was surprised at how my deep-rooted beliefs impacted my entire life. I had so many painful past experiences that were influencing my behavior and everyday life. What astonished me the most was the fact that I had these beliefs subconsciously and did not realize them or the impact they had on my behavior and the decisions I made.

Slowly, I began my self-healing journey once again. During this process, I discovered the negative beliefs I had about love, trust, security, career, and finances. Fast forward to today, and I have learned so much about my inner child. My relationship with myself and my partner is not completely perfect. However, I am in a better place now than I was back then. I continue to practice inner child healing every day and learn something new about my inner child each time. I have learned to embrace my essence and understand myself better.

Through practicing inner child healing, I have gained so much resilience, joy, peace, calm, and self-love. I hope that as I share my experience with you in this book, you will find healing, overcome emotional pain, and create balance in your life.

As you begin to learn about the concept outlined in this book, it may sound weird at first. I ask that you keep an open mind and let your curiosity and intuition guide you. When I first heard about inner child healing, I found the concept strange, and I did not entirely believe in it until I started practicing it.

Inner child healing is a concept that is psychologically proven, and you do not have to be spiritual to practice the concept.

Chapter 1: The Inner Child Healing Concept

The internal war you wage with yourself may not be seen by others, but is always felt by you! – Lorraine Dawn Nilon

When you think about your childhood, what comes to mind? We all have different memories of our childhood—the places we grew up in, the people we were surrounded by, the friends we made, and the places we visited. Some of these memories play out quite clearly on your mind's screen. Others, however, may have become blurred over time.

When you go back into your past, what do you recall first? Perhaps you are reminded of the family vacations you took and the exciting adventures you embarked on that brought your family closer. Or, maybe you are reminded of the summer camps you attended, the friends you made during your school days, your favorite teacher who was your biggest cheerleader, and all the school awards you took home for academic excellence.

While you may have had wonderful experiences growing up, some of them may not have been so pleasant. For example, you may have witnessed family arguments, had problems with other kids at school, experienced sibling rivalry, or experienced some other form of tragedy in your life. All these experiences had an impact on your psychological development as a child. They shaped the way you think, how you see yourself, and your perspective on other people.

A wounded inner child often results from specific events that happened in your past such as bullying, being criticized, or losing a loved one but, it can also be a result of things you never experienced. For example, if your caregivers failed to make you feel loved, it is probable that you still feel unloved. Or, someone who has difficulty setting and respecting boundaries may have grown up with parents or caregivers who failed to set and reinforce boundaries for them. If a certain behavior was never modeled to you from childhood, it is difficult to adapt the behavior as you grow older.

What Is Inner Child Healing?

To gain a better understanding of the inner child healing concept, let us first define what the inner child is. Psychologists and medical experts define the inner child as an internal mental health complex that exists in all of us (ReGain, 2023). In analytical psychology, the "inner child" is described as a person's childlike aspect. It is the sum of what we learn from infancy right into adolescence. The inner child can also be defined as the self-governing subpersonality that exists beneath the conscious mind.

When we think of trauma, we often think of extremely traumatizing and horrible experiences such as natural disasters, physical and sexual assault, or witnessing the death of a loved one, but these are not the only incidents that cause trauma. Often, experiences that may seem harmless from an adult's perspective, such as failing to meet a child's emotional needs, can have a major emotional and psychological impact on a child.

Everyone has an inner child. But what separates us from our childhood? Is it age, perhaps? Or, our experiences?

Most people would say it is both—which is true, but we are separated from our childhood when we stop using our imagination and expressing ourselves through our creativity. As we grow older, we stop imagining the endless possibilities of who and what we can become. Instead, we allow our past experiences to dictate how we should live our lives.

Imagine for a second that you are six years old, and you are at your friend's birthday party, playing in the garden with other kids. You are running around flying a paper kite—innocent, carefree, and having fun. You then stumble onto a chair and fall. With bruised elbows and knees, you begin to cry. Instead of helping you up, the other kids laugh at you. As an adult, you may not remember every detail of that event. You may not even remember what color clothes you were wearing or the names of the other kids at the party. But, the memory that you are likely to remember is the pain and humiliation you felt when the other kids laughed at you. This particular experience may have led you to convince yourself never to put yourself out there again. Twenty or thirty years after this painful experience, you find yourself with social anxiety and unable to connect with your peers.

Your physical wounds may have healed, and you may have forgotten about what happened in the past. However, this experience left an emotional wound that still runs your life. Your six-year-old self dictates how you live your life.

While shying away from social situations may protect you from getting hurt again, it also prevents you from taking risks and living life to your fullest potential. It holds you back from meeting new people, learning new cultures and languages, and pursuing new adventures.

The inner child healing concept involves reconnecting with the innermost parts of yourself. It recognizes that we live our lives based on our childhood experiences and brings awareness to our unmet needs.

Inner child healing allows you to heal past trauma—both conscious and unconscious. Through reparenting, the concept allows you to address your unmet childhood emotional needs. In today's world, we often look to change the symptoms of a problem instead of addressing the root cause. However, sustainable change only comes when we address the challenges we face, such as emotional issues and mental health conditions, from the root. The concept of inner child healing allows us to dive into the past and uncover our beliefs about love, ourselves, relationships, money, careers, and the world around us. The main objective of inner child healing is to work with the wounded inner child to strengthen the adult self.

By reaching into the deepest parts of your psyche and healing your past pain, you learn to reconnect with your creative side and find joy and meaning in life. Healing your wounded inner child is a lifelong process and requires patience, empathy, and self-awareness. It is a journey of self-discovery that helps us understand our core behaviors, triggers, needs, and wants. When we heal the wounded inner child, we become receptive and open ourselves to new possibilities. We become both the healed child and the adult who is empathetic and compassionate—who is able to give and receive love.

The Two Parts of the Inner Child

Children are born innocent, untainted, and full of life. That first cry a baby makes—through their tiny lungs when they arrive in this world—is a sign of life and the child's ability to express his or her emotions. Within each of us is an inner child who is innocent, cheerful, creative, sensitive, curious, playful, optimistic, and believes in endless possibilities but also holds the accumulated pain, fears, and traumas from childhood experiences. We carry within us the wounded inner child and the healed inner child—the child we were before we experienced trauma.

We have the ability to be creative, mindful, patient, and authentic. However, through our experiences, we developed certain behaviors as a way to cope with emotional pain. We learned to hide our natural abilities behind these coping mechanisms and somehow lost sight of our true essence. The goal of inner child healing is to heal the wounded inner child and reconnect you with the healed inner child, who is unafraid and has no shame in who he or she is.

The Symptoms of a Wounded Inner Child

Every child born into this world has the right to and deserves safety, security, and protection. However, this is not always the case for some children. It is every parent's or caregiver's responsibility to ensure that a child grows up in a safe environment where all their basic needs are met. Children's basic needs include safety, stability, emotional support, love, education, access to medical care, food, clean water, and shelter. Sadly, not all parents recognize, are aware of, and have the ability to fulfill that responsibility. Protecting a child does not just mean keeping them physically safe. It means protecting a child's emotional and psychological well-being as well. When a child does not feel safe and protected in the environment they grow up in, they experience deep emotional wounds that show up later in adulthood as repressed emotions.

Pretending that emotional pain does not exist does not make it disappear into thin air. Past wounds have a way of resurfacing in adulthood as frustration in relationships, being unable to meet your own needs, low self-esteem, and the inability to give and receive love, among other things.

Childhood emotional wounds can also resurface in adulthood as immature behavior, issues with setting and respecting boundaries, rage, mood swings, and challenges connecting with your partner in an intimate relationship. They can manifest as post-traumatic disorder, aggressive behavior, emotional unavailability, or self-image issues. For example, if you experienced childhood emotional neglect, you may find it difficult to connect with other people emotionally. Your inability to process and deal with your own emotions can prevent you from nurturing the emotions of others.

Left unresolved, childhood emotional trauma can make it difficult to function as a responsible, empathetic, loving, and self-aware adult. Life becomes a rollercoaster of emotional ups and downs. It becomes close to impossible to live a fulfilling life when you still suffer from childhood emotional traumas.

The following are signs of a wounded inner child:

- You are unable to give and receive love.
- You have destructive and compulsive behavior such as anger, workaholism, or substance and drug abuse.
- You feel like something is wrong with you and you are not good enough.
- You neglect your own needs.
- You become anxious when engaging in something new.
- You are ashamed of how you feel and so, you hide your true feelings.
- You do not trust others, which leads to controlling behavior.
- You are afraid of failure.
- You criticize yourself and judge yourself harshly.
- You hide your authentic self or have an inflated ego.
- You use emotions instead of logical thinking which often leads to impulsive reactions such as slamming doors, yelling, and other eruptive behavior.

- You lack boundaries or feel bad for setting them.
- You are a people pleaser.
- You are unstable and change work, friendships, and partners often.
- You are a compulsive caretaker.
- You feel lonely more often than usual which results from the experience of not being understood or feeling left abandoned.
- You prefer to be invisible and often avoid conflict and confrontation.
- You are dissatisfied with your body.
- You are a perfectionist and believe that self-worth is defined by productivity and success.
- You are passive.

Healing starts with an awareness of the things that caused you pain. When you acknowledge your inner child and heal your emotional wounds, you start seeing life through an optimistic lens. It allows you to rediscover your positive attributes and unlock your natural gifts and talents. Avoiding doing the inner work needed to heal emotional trauma often leads to destructive and compulsive behavior such as anger, workaholism, or substance and drug abuse.

In the next chapter, we will explore more and gain a better understanding of how a wounded inner child affects your life and the importance of healing past trauma.

Chapter 2: Is Your Inner Child Running Your Life?

Inside of each of us is just an inner child yearning to love and be loved in return.
–Soul Works

Do you find yourself in conflicts with family, friends, colleagues, or your partner more often than usual? Do you sometimes feel like no matter how hard you try to get different results in your relationships, you still end up with the same negative, frustrating results? If your answers are yes to both questions, perhaps it is time to explore how your inner child is running your life and find effective ways to resolve your emotional issues.

Imagine for a second a ten-year-old who wakes up every day and commutes to his job to earn a living just so he or she can provide for his family. That sounds absurd, right? Yet many of us still make decisions and live our lives based on the experiences of our ten-year-old selves.

You may have noticed that you experience fear, anxiety, anger, perfectionism, and codependency. These are ways your inner child seeks to feel safe.

When your wounded inner child is in control of your life, it will choose unconscious thoughts, behaviors, and beliefs that result from your childhood experiences. Your inner child does not have adult experience and cannot comprehend that your life has changed and that you have a different life experience.

How Your Inner Child Affects Your Life

Emotional And Mental Wellbeing

The thing about emotional pain is that it does not just disappear with time by ignoring the fact that it exists. Unfortunately, the past does not always remain in the past, where it belongs, as we normally say. Psychological pain can intensely affect all areas of your life. It can manifest itself in your behaviors in adulthood.

While most people think that emotional wounds have far less impact on us than physical wounds, emotional pain can result in feelings that impact your physical and mental health, such as low self-esteem, anxiety, chronic fatigue, stress, and depression. This can significantly affect your ability to function as an adult. I had a strong core belief that I was not good enough, and I was always triggered when something did not work out the way I wanted it to. At university, I often struggled during times when I was preparing for my exams. I remember struggling with an exercise one time. I got extremely upset and frustrated with myself, to the point of throwing my books on the floor. The problem was never the exercise I was working on but my core belief that I was not good enough and the immense self-doubt that worked hand in hand with my limiting beliefs.

By placing your wounded inner child in the driver's seat, you allow yourself to go through the same pain over and over again, and when triggers appear, your response to those triggers is often very overwhelming.

Relationships

Are you always caught up in arguments with your partner? Do you use manipulation to get people to do what you want, and is everything either your way or the highway—with no room for compromise? These are ways in which the inner child causes us to act immaturely, which often results in conflicts in relationships.

A wounded inner child can cause havoc in your relationships. It unconsciously recreates your past experiences and projects the roles of your parents, caregivers, and everyone else you grew up around onto your current relationships. What your inner child needs is for you to meet your unmet childhood needs in your present life. For example, if your parents criticized you a lot as a child, in adulthood you may find that you analyze people's voices, behaviors, or body language to find signs of criticism. Even when love is present in your relationships, what you hear the most are the projections of your wounded inner child—the voice of criticism that keeps telling you that you are not good enough.

I often reacted emotionally to any kind of constructive criticism—from my partner, my parents, and anyone else who was trying to reason with me. Each time someone would say, "Milena, I think you have to go through your work again because there are a lot of mistakes." My brain interpreted it as "You are not good enough," and therefore, my reaction towards the situation would often be very emotional, which led to escalated tensions and arguments. The people in my life often felt misunderstood, and that put a strain on my relationships.

Childhood traumas often affect our feelings of trust, safety, recognition, and autonomy, and these are key elements in building and maintaining healthy relationships. For so long, I had challenges making deeper connections with people. I felt isolated and lonely, although I was surrounded by a lot of loving and supportive people. For some reason, I did not feel connected to people at a deeper level and could not open up to anyone. These feelings were a result of my belief that no one would like me for who I am if I showed my vulnerable side.

Unresolved trauma can affect your self-esteem and the way you relate to other people. For example, when I was about five years old, my family lived in an apartment building. There were two families who also had children my age on the floor above ours. We would sometimes run into each other in the elevator, and I remember desperately wanting to be their friend. I thought they looked pretty. They always wore fashionable clothes and accessories that made me envious.

One day, our mothers arranged a playdate for the three of us. Finally, I had an opportunity to go to the neighbor's apartment one Saturday morning. Upon arrival, one of the moms welcomed me into their home; the two girls were already playing in the living room when I arrived. After introducing us to each other, the moms went into the kitchen to chat. I was left alone with the two girls, who did not seem interested in being friends with me. To break the awkwardness, I decided to ask them what they were doing, but they ignored me. I then asked if I could join in the game and play with them, and they both laughed at me.

Just ten minutes after arriving at our playdate, one of the girls told me to go home.

“Tell your mom that you don’t feel good,” she said.

The other added, “Maybe we’ll be in the mood tomorrow if you bring us a toy to play with.”

So I did as they instructed. I went into the kitchen and told my mother that I had an upset stomach. We said our goodbyes and left.

The following morning, I asked my mother if I could go to the neighbor’s apartment again, and she gave me permission. This time, I brought my favorite toy to impress the girls. When I arrived there, they said the same thing, “Come back again tomorrow and bring a different toy,” they told me. This repeated five more times before I gave up.

To an adult, this may seem like a harmless situation. The girls did not say anything particularly mean to me, but the way they dismissed me made me feel like I was not good enough to be part of their circle. I thought to myself that maybe if I had better toys, they would have been interested in playing with me. Or perhaps if I had worn better clothes, they would have thought I was pretty enough to be their friend. The belief that I was not good enough the way I was was a result of some of the painful experiences I went through as a child.

In those formative years, I questioned my self-worth. I continued to doubt myself whenever I met new people. For years, the prevailing thought in my head was that "if I'm slim, beautiful, and successful, people will like me."

A wounded inner child can deeply affect your relationships with others, and even worse, it can affect your relationship with yourself. It impacts your emotional and mental well-being.

Healing is a process and requires patience and continuous effort from you. While doing the inner work, keep the following ideas in mind:

1. Emotional wounds have a way of resurfacing in the future through our behaviors. Therefore, it is important to address the unresolved emotional issues you may have.

2. A wounded inner child seeks to meet your childhood unmet needs. It unconsciously

recreates your past experiences by projecting the roles caregivers played in your childhood into your current relationships. If left unresolved, this can affect how you relate to others and leads to toxic behavior in your relationships.

3. Unresolved trauma can lead to low self-esteem and prevent you from living life to your full potential.

4. Childhood emotional wounds affect your feelings of trust, sense of security, recognition, and autonomy and these are key elements to building and maintaining healthy relationships.

Having a clear understanding of where your emotional pain stems from and the exact cause is the first step to healing past trauma. When you are aware of the areas in your life you need to work on, you allow yourself to do the work and seek the necessary help you need to enhance your life.

In the following chapter, we will learn about what causes a wounded inner child and bring awareness to some of the unconscious past experiences that often trigger emotional pain in adulthood.

Chapter 3: Causes of a Wounded Inner Child

Growing up is not just about moving forward, but also an endless cycle of returning to our childhood wonders and wounds. –Silvery Afternoon

Going back into your past to find out where the emotional issues you are facing stem from is never an easy thing to do. It triggers a lot of painful memories, but it is an important step in your healing process. Most of the mental and emotional issues we are facing are a result of our past experiences. Our behaviors are a result of the beliefs we developed from our experiences. Whatever you missed out on growing up—love, attention, affection, and emotional stability—your wounded inner child seeks to fulfill in adulthood.

So, let us have a look at how beliefs are formed.

How Beliefs Are Formed

While school provides academic education from an early age to help us adapt to society, most of what we learn we gather from our parents and caregivers, who guide us from infancy on how to live and behave in society. Science shows that learning starts during the last trimester of pregnancy. This is the time when a fetus learns about the world through the mother's responses, in the form of an increase in cortisol (the stress hormone) or an increase in dopamine (the feel-good hormone).

In early childhood, a child starts to learn by observing and mimicking the behaviors of the people they grow up with.

A child's brain develops at a fast rate from the time they are born up until the age of five—more than at any other time of their life. In his 2019 book, *The Biology of Belief*, Dr. Bruce Lipton explains how our minds develop beliefs in the subconscious in early childhood. From the ages of zero to seven years, the human brain mainly functions at theta and alpha wave frequencies—the same frequencies you are in when under hypnosis or in a deep meditation state. This part of the brain is responsible for learning, creativity, memory, and intuition.

Everything that a child learns during this phase of their development goes unfiltered into their subconscious mind. To a child, there is no difference between imagination and the real world.

In early childhood, a child does not have the ability or experience to reason and think rationally. Their little minds accept whatever they are told as truth. This stage is critical in the development of a child's mind. This is the time when the subconscious is programmed and a belief system is formed.

The subconscious can be likened to a computer hard drive. It is the central storage bank for the information fed into the brain. Now, imagine operating a computer with software that was developed and installed over three decades ago and has never been upgraded. How would it function? Would it be as efficient as the latest version? It would not, right? Yet most of us are operating on outdated software and information that was programmed in us when we were kids.

Your subconscious controls the conscious part of brain activity. Ninety-five percent of the time, we operate from the subconscious and function consciously only five percent of the time. What this means is that most of your behaviors are automatic responses—without conscious control. For example, if your core belief is "I am not good enough," and this belief is deep down in your subconscious mind, you will automatically base a lot of your decisions on that core belief without even realizing it.

The Montessori Theory

In her book, *The Absorbent Mind*, Maria Montessori, an Italian physician, and educator, explains the inner workings of a child's mind. According to Montessori, a child relates differently to his or her environment compared to an adult (1995). At the age of six, a child's brain absorbs all the information in their environment. This is a continuous process that happens effortlessly for every child.

Children do not only remember the things they see and hear. The information they absorb forms part of their souls. They embody everything they are exposed to.

A child's brain is programmed to learn at a fast rate. Think of what a child accomplishes in the first seven years of their life—learning verbal and non-verbal communication, gross motor skills, and social and emotional skills. For an adult, it would take about six years of hard work to learn what a child can learn in their first three years.

By the time a child turns five years old, they will have developed eighty-five percent of their brain structure. All this is achieved through the "absorbent mind." Montessori further explains in her book that in the absorbent mind stage, a child establishes their individuality and builds an identity for who they will become as an adult. At this stage of development, a child understands the difference between children and adults, but they cannot comprehend that adults can make mistakes. Children are very egocentric, and if something unfavorable happens around them, they feel that it is their fault and often internalize that experience. For example, if a parent has to put in long hours at work and always comes home late and does not spend much time with them, a child will automatically think that it is because of him or her. The child will believe that he or she did something wrong and that is the reason why their mom or dad does not spend time with them. Children simply do not have the experience to understand that such incidents have nothing to do with them.

Growing up, I was in acting school. I loved to entertain people and perform little acts; the one person I wanted to show my acting skills to was my mother. However, my mom did not always have the time to attend my school plays, and that really upset me. At the time, my little brain could not fully comprehend what was going on—I did not understand that she had to work, and most of the time, it was because of her job that she could not attend my school plays. To the child in me, this meant that my performance was not good enough and that I was not good enough to receive any attention.

Childhood is a very vulnerable time, and everything that a child experiences forms part of his or her belief system. We carry these experiences and beliefs into adulthood and often pay less attention to how they affect us. As adults, we all have that part within us that has not grown up. The part that experienced pain and never healed—the wounded inner child.

Many of us see the world through the eyes of our wounded inner child. This is why we often feel strong feelings of anger, fear, self-doubt, and powerlessness. If your belief, based on your childhood experience, was that you were not good enough, it is highly likely that you still have this belief programmed deep down in your subconscious as an adult. Your behavior and how you feel about yourself are influenced by this belief.

Beliefs are not only formed through what people say to you but also from other people's perspectives about life, their jobs, their relationships, their money, and even their physical appearance. For example, my mother always criticized the way she looked and was frustrated by her body weight. Growing up, I developed the belief that to be beautiful and accepted, you had to be slim. This belief resulted in my eating disorder and dissatisfaction with my body.

Our beliefs influence our decisions and choices and how we live our lives. They are the bridge between where you are and where you would like to be in life. They can either hold you back or catapult you to the next level of your life. Most of us live in fear of pursuing our dreams, not because we do not have what it takes to achieve success, but because we believe what the little voice in our heads tells us—that we are not good enough or talented enough to pursue our dreams. So, we shrink back and live our entire adult lives in the back seat, not realizing our full potential. We allow fear to paralyze us and would rather remain in our comfort zone than confront the emotional struggles we are facing.

You can be anything you choose to be. Often, we say things like, "I have always been like this." No one is born afraid; we learn about fear from somewhere or from someone. No one is born insecure, believing that they are ugly, unworthy, and unlovable. The information we have today, which we learned through our experiences, can be replaced with new information by embracing healing and opening ourselves to new experiences.

Five Typical Childhood Wounds

The experiences we went through in childhood may differ, but the effects are present for everyone. As you grow up, you may forget some details of your childhood, such as the first time you learned to walk or your first day in kindergarten. However, it is difficult to forget a painful experience, such as when other kids in school teased or bullied you. And even when you do, these childhood emotional wounds are still present in adulthood and directly affect how we relate to others. They produce fear and a lack of trust, preventing you from building and maintaining healthy relationships. The following are the five most common childhood emotional wounds that hold people back from living up to their full potential.

Fear of Abandonment

Most of us have experienced abandonment at some point in our lives. Whether it is your best friend who abandoned you for the cool kids in school or a parent who left you to be raised by family members, this kind of experience often results in feelings of abandonment and the fear of rejection.

When you have suffered abandonment as a child, your coping mechanism is often to create barriers to prevent anyone from coming closer to you. You continue to carry the fear of abandonment into adulthood and live your life believing that if you let people in, they may hurt you. Because of the fear of abandonment, some people are afraid of being alone and often jump from one relationship to another—even when the relationship is not healthy for them. They often develop unhealthy behaviors in relationships, such as jealousy and clinginess, and cannot set boundaries.

Fear of Rejection

The fear of rejection is often caused by parents, siblings, family members, or peers. This emotional wound impedes you from processing your feelings, thoughts, and experiences. It tends to prevent a child from developing a healthy sense of self. This is one of the causes of low self-esteem and self-acceptance.

A person who suffered rejection as a child often struggles with self-love, thoughts of being unwanted, and looking down on themselves. They feel unworthy of love, and the fear of re-experiencing rejection again drives them to isolate themselves.

Fear of Humiliation

The fear of humiliation results from receiving harsh criticism and disapproval from others. This is most common in people who were accused of clumsiness and told they were stupid, bad, immature, overweight, and called all kinds of mean words. This not only destroys a child's self-esteem but also prevents them from developing self-worth. If left unresolved, the fear of humiliation can manifest itself in adulthood in the form of dependent behavior and a deep feeling of having done things wrong or that something is wrong with you.

Betrayal

The fear of betrayal is quite common among people who were betrayed by the people they trusted, such as parents, caregivers, family members, teachers, or neighbors. Feelings of betrayal result when someone you trusted breaks the promises they made to you. This causes feelings of being cheated and often leads to distrust, envy, and feeling like you do not deserve what others have to offer.

Experiencing betrayal in childhood often results in controlling behavior and perfectionism in adulthood. To gain a sense of control, people who were betrayed growing up feel they need to be strict and have control over others. This is a coping mechanism they developed to prevent getting disappointed.

Injustice

Often, children who are raised by parents or caregivers who are authoritative and stern grow up feeling powerless and incompetent. Being raised by someone with a demanding personality often results in a rigid personality in adulthood. Most times, people who suffered injustice growing up can achieve great success; however, their need for order and perfectionism, as well as their radical thinking, can get in the way of making sound decisions.

Injustice can also be a result of growing up in a society with racial discrimination, violence, bullying, and being falsely criticized. Experiencing this kind of injustice in childhood often leads to low self-esteem and self-worth. It creates feelings of hopelessness and is linked to mental health conditions such as anxiety and depression.

Injustice wounds trigger anger, irritability, and aggressiveness and can make you feel unsafe and insecure in your relationships. Working on healing the wounds of injustice can help you be more flexible toward others. I can also help you learn to trust people more.

Awareness Exercise:

Write down the emotional wounds you identify with and your behaviors associated with each emotional wound. For example, if you were criticized as a child and grew up to be a perfectionist, you can write: injustice wound—false criticism; behavior—perfectionism, rigid thinking, lack of trust, feelings of guilt and shame.

Later on in this book, we will return to this list to identify the core beliefs that are at the center of your decision-making process.

Being aware of your emotional wounds can help you come up with effective ways to heal them. As you practice the above exercise, keep the following in mind:

- Most of the core beliefs that run your life were formed in your subconscious between the ages of zero to seven years.
- The subconscious is part of the brain that records all our experiences—it is the central storage bank that keeps all the information fed into the brain.
- As a child, you had little ability and experience to comprehend some of the experiences you went through and most of these experiences were not your fault.
- Ninety-five percent of the time, as adults, we function from the subconscious, and our responses are automatic and not consciously controlled.
- The most common emotional wounds that hold people from living to their full potential are the fear of rejection, fear of abandonment, fear of humiliation, fear of betrayal, and injustice.
- These wounds are a result of your childhood experiences and influence your decisions, your choices, your self-image, and your relationships.
- Childhood emotional wounds manifest themselves in adulthood as behaviors such

as low self-esteem and low self-worth, difficulty trusting others, dependent behavior, and perfectionism among other behavior patterns.

In the next chapter, we will learn how to begin doing the inner work and connecting with your inner child to find healing and create a new belief system.

Chapter 4: Connecting With Your Inner Child

After a while, the middle-aged person who lives in her head begins to talk to her soul, the kid. –Joe Jones

Often, when we are encouraged to do the inner work, our first response is fear of what may come up when we dig up the past. You never know exactly what to expect. The experience of connecting with your inner child for the first time is different for everyone. For some people, it can be an overwhelming experience, and for others, it can be quite liberating.

The first time I connected with my inner child, I discovered where my insecurities about my body came from. I had the belief that I was not good enough, so as I grew up, I became a perfectionist. This was my way of making up for how I felt about myself. To gain a sense of self-worth, my work had to be absolutely perfect—with no mistakes. If I could not figure something out during my studies, I got extremely frustrated and angry at myself.

The core beliefs we have about ourselves influence our behaviors. You may not even realize how much they impact your life until you become aware of them. As you begin your healing process, it is important to remember that you had no control over some of your experiences. We often hold onto past wounds and feelings of guilt because of what we experienced in the past—you may even believe that you were quite a handful, annoying, and flawed. These beliefs may be the reason you feel insecure and anxious about what others think of you. However, the truth is that every child is unique in their own way and deserves to grow up in an environment that allows them to express their individuality. It is unfortunate that no one noticed your natural gifts and talents; however, it is not too late to start believing in yourself.

The past has important lessons for us to learn from. We have developed resilience and strength of character from our past experiences. Without these experiences, there can be no growth. However, holding on to past pain only stunts your growth and keeps you stuck in self-limiting beliefs that stifle your potential. You can break through the behavior patterns that are holding you back and create a beautiful, better future for yourself.

In her book, *How To Do The Work*, Dr. Nicole LePera, a holistic psychologist, explains how to identify your inner child (2021). Growing up, we develop coping mechanisms that help us navigate our way through challenging times. These coping mechanisms help us get through overwhelming situations, but they also conceal our emotional pain instead of dealing with the root cause. Unresolved emotional wounds often resurface in adulthood as fear, self-doubt, and negative thoughts. Dr. LePera describes these thoughts and feelings that make us feel like what we offer this world is not enough as inner child archetypes.

The Seven Inner Child Archetypes

Your inner child is the unconscious part of your adult self. It is the part of you that you may not be aware of and that shows up in your life as emotions you were not allowed to express as a child, such as guilt and shame, or unmet needs, such as safety and stability.

As we grow into adults, we assume that every part of us is growing and we are developing healthy patterns; however, that is not always the case. Most of us are still seeing the world through the eyes of our younger selves. A child does not have the experience to understand what it feels like to be an adult. Children use their feelings more than they do logic. They give meaning to every situation—even those that have nothing to do with them. Most of us still operate from a wounded inner child's perspective—in our relationships, careers, and in life in general. This is why we often get stuck in old patterns, and no matter how hard we try to break through self-limiting beliefs, we often end up in the same place as before—frustrated and disappointed by our results. According to Dr. LePera, the inner child archetypes are thinking and behavior patterns we develop from our childhood experiences. The seven childhood archetypes are:

- The Overachiever
- The Caretaker
- The Underachiever
- The Rescuer or Protector
- The Yes-person
- The Life of the party
- The Hero-worshiper

The Overachiever

An overachiever uses external validation such as academic, career, or material success as a coping mechanism against low self-esteem. The need to overachieve also applies to their relationships. Overachievers believe that to receive love, they must achieve some level of success, and they do not want to disappoint the people they love.

The Caretaker

People with this inner child archetype gain a sense of self-worth by taking care of other people's needs at the expense of their own. The caretaker is often overly caring and will put the needs of others first. This archetype is common in people who did not experience unconditional love as children and the assurance that adults are there to take care of them. They believe that to be loved, you need to take care of others.

The Underachiever

Underachievers believe that to be loved, you must be invisible and not stand out or compete with others. Therefore, they keep themselves unseen and hide their potential out of fear of criticism and failure. Often, these people put much focus on achievement when they were younger.

The Rescuer Or Protector

The rescuer always tries to protect, help, or save those around them as a way to cope with their vulnerability. This gives them power, control, and a sense of worth. The rescuer believes that people cannot cope on their own and that in order to be loved, you need to help solve their problems.

The Yes-person

The yes-person simply cannot say "No" to others. They are self-sacrificing and would do anything to help other people. They would rather deny themselves what they need than say "No" when someone asks for something. Often, the yes-person went through the experience of taking care of others from a young age and therefore learned to put other people's needs ahead of their own. At the core of this belief is a deep need to earn love.

The Life of the party

The life of the party person believes they always need to be cheerful. They never show their vulnerable side often because, as children, they were ashamed of showing their true emotions.

The Hero-worshiper

The hero-worshiper seeks to have someone they idolize and will do anything to be accepted by that person. Often, this need for codependency stems from having been raised by someone who appeared to be perfect and had no fault. This experience resulted in the belief that, in order to be loved, they needed to emulate the success of their idol or someone they admire. Before making any decision, the hero-worshiper often asks the opinion of others and does not believe in themselves or their ideas.

Uncovering Your Beliefs

Each inner child archetype experienced some sort of trauma in the past and has childhood needs that were never met. In adulthood, we play our family system roles. These roles were modeled to us, and we unconsciously assumed some of them as a means of survival; they now form part of our belief system. Your personality traits are beliefs about yourself that you have developed from childhood.

Often, we say to ourselves, "I am not good enough," "I cannot have this," or "I am dumb and just cannot get things right." These negative thoughts build up over time and become part of your belief system. Your belief system informs your decisions and influences the choices you make. Thoughts contribute to feelings of depression, and depression is often a sign of deeper emotional issues. Leaving past emotional wounds unresolved is a great price to pay for things that happened in the past—which, for the most part, you had no control over. In order to quiet the voice of your inner critic, you must acknowledge your wounded inner child and the negative beliefs that have been running your life.

Healing begins when we understand the underlying causes of our wounds. Perhaps as a child, you felt powerless, but that does not mean you are powerless and hopeless today as an adult. Living the rest of your life believing that you are hopeless will only prevent you from realizing your full potential.

Developmental Trauma Beliefs And How They Affect Your Life

Traumatic experiences make us see life through the lens of pain. When our sense of safety is destroyed, we change our perspective and find ways to adapt to our environment. Developmental trauma beliefs are the result of a series of childhood traumatic experiences that affect a child's development. Someone who grew up being criticized and falsely accused of things they did not do is an example of this. As an adult, it is likely that this person will develop negative beliefs about themselves and see themselves as an incompetent and unlovable person.

Negative beliefs often lead to maladaptive behaviors such as compulsive behavior, which can cause mental health conditions and relationship problems.

When doing inner work, it is important to do a self-evaluation from time to time. It will help you be more aware of your negative beliefs and how they are holding you back.

The following are the most common developmental trauma beliefs most of us carry into adulthood.

"I Cannot Trust Others"

A person who was betrayed and had their trust broken as a child by parents or caregivers often struggles with trusting or relying on people. Because they were betrayed by people close to them at a time when they were vulnerable, they tend to develop a fear of rejection and abandonment. In adulthood, they continue to operate out of this fear even when circumstances are different and are certainly not related to the past. This often leads to an obsession with self-reliance. Their inability to rely on other people tends to prevent them from asking for or accepting help—even when they need it.

This negative belief often leads to depression, codependency, and loneliness. It is also the cause of having an unhealthy relationship with yourself and with others.

"The World Is A Dangerous Place"

When a child is raised by emotionally unstable and inconsistent parents or caregivers, they grow up believing that the world is an unsafe place to be and that their well-being is in danger. This results in the child developing the belief that they are helpless. Often, this kind of trauma leaves a child feeling anxious, and their behavior is driven by fear. Living a fear-based life results in the brain developing ways to over-process the information in your environment. It can cause you to feel edgy and unsafe.

Anxiety and fear can result in low self-esteem and a lack of motivation to work on improving your life. It can get in the way of your academic, personal, and professional success. Living in fear and anxiety often makes a person inaccessible, distant, and difficult–which can cause problems in relationships. It also prevents you from taking risks, making the necessary changes, standing up for yourself, and creating new habits to help improve your life.

“I Am Unlovable”

When a child grows up in an environment where they are constantly ignored and their feelings are invalidated, they grow up believing that their feelings are not important and they are not worthy. A child has no ability or experience to separate their parents’ bad attitudes from their own self-worth. When a parent or caregiver is angry, the child will typically assume it is because of them.

Other common negative beliefs are:

- Nobody understands me.
- My feelings do not matter.
- I am inferior.
- I am powerless.

- There is something wrong with me.
- I am not beautiful.
- I do not fit anywhere.
- I have to make others happy.
- The people I love always abandon me.
- I'm always to blame.
- I am small.
- I am a burden.
- I am not allowed to defend myself.
- I am worthless.
- I cannot show emotions.
- I am not important.

Often, these feelings of inadequateness lead people who grew up feeling ignored to work hard to get noticed and feel accepted. Their self-esteem is low, so they tend to use personal achievement to gain a sense of self-worth. They often become perfectionists, people-pleasers, and codependent. The fear of rejection drives them to be the yes-person who is always there to help others.

It takes courage and patience to work on your negative beliefs. If you identify with the developmental beliefs above, you can recognize when negative thoughts start to creep in and counter them with positive, uplifting ones. Be intentional in your healing process, and remember not to take everything that happens to you personally. What we call reality is actually a compilation of knowledge from the past that is organized through our belief systems. The emotional significance you attach to your past experiences determines how you respond to future situations but does not always equate to fact or reality.

The following exercises will help identify your core beliefs.

Exercise 1: Get to Know Your Core Beliefs

1. Set your timer to one hour and write down everything you believe about yourself and the world.

2. Stay focused. It may happen that you do not recall all your beliefs at once but, stay focused, I guarantee that you will find other beliefs that lie hidden, deep in your psyche.

3. After an hour, read through your beliefs and write down three to six things your core beliefs have in common. It could be that they stem from the fear of rejection or from feelings of guilt and shame.

Exercise 2: Be Curious and Ask Yourself Questions

- Ask yourself why you believe these things to be true about yourself.
- What annoys you?
- What is the quickest way to get you upset?
- When do you feel most stressed and why?
- What makes you feel trapped and stuck, and why?
- In what moments do you feel most frustrated?

Exercise 3: Be Mindful Of Your Triggers

A trigger is anything that elicits an emotional response. It could be a person, place, or situation. Often, it is an intense emotional reaction to a situation. For example, someone may be triggered by public speaking. They may feel sweaty and anxious, and their heart rate may increase when they stand in front of a crowd.

Identifying your triggers can help you take note of what they are linked to. To identify your triggers;

- Notice how you feel.
    - Do you feel anxious and overwhelmed?
    - Do you feel upset?
    - Do you feel anger?
    - Do you have difficulty calming yourself down?
- Next, ask yourself why you feel the way you do.
    - Is there something weighing on your mind?
    - Is it something of significance or repeat negative thoughts?
- Listen to yourself.
    - What thoughts keep coming up in your mind?

- Does your mind keep playing a particular scene from a past event?

Exercise 4:

1. In your journal, draw a picture of a little girl or boy you envision as your younger self.
2. Go over the four typical childhood wounds discussed in Chapter 3 and note which ones you identify with.
3. Next, identify your inner child archetype.
4. Write down the feelings and emotions that come up during this exercise.
5. What core beliefs did you identify in the first exercise?
6. What lessons did you draw from the second exercise?
7. Identify your triggers and ask yourself why you are emotionally triggered by them.
8. Write everything down on that picture of the girl or boy.

Keep your journal safe. Each time you want to do the healing exercises, look at the drawing of the little girl or boy—it will help you reconnect with your wounded inner child.

As you go through your healing journey, remember that the objective of the inner child healing concept is to help you connect with and heal the psychological and emotional part of you that experienced trauma. To help you gain a better understanding of your inner child, keep the following ideas in mind.

- There are seven inner child archetypes to help you identify your inner child, as described by Dr. Nicole LePera:

    - The overachiever: uses personal achievement to validate themselves and to gain a sense of self-worth.

    - The caretaker: believes in order to be loved they need to take care of the needs of others even if it means putting theirs last.

    - The underachiever: believes they have to play small and not stand out among other people because of fear of rejection or failure.

    - The rescuer or protector: believes in saving and protecting others as a way to hide their own vulnerability.

    - The yes-person: believes that they must sacrifice what they have for others even if it means denying themselves what they need.
    - The life of the party: never shows his or her vulnerable side often they are ashamed of showing their true emotions.
    - And, the hero-worshiper: has the need to poll people before making decisions about their life and does not trust themselves and their ideas.
- Your experiences shape your worldview and form your belief system.
- Your personality traits are beliefs you developed about yourself from childhood.
- Developmental trauma beliefs result from a series of childhood traumatic experiences.
- These beliefs impact your decisions, life choices, and how you perceive yourself and relate with others,
- Common trauma beliefs are beliefs such as "I am unlovable," "I cannot trust people," "I am powerless," "I am a burden," "My feelings do

not matter," or "The world is a dangerous place."

- Identifying your core beliefs can help you note when negative thoughts creep in and it allows you to replace them with positive, uplifting ones.

Healing your inner child is beneficial not only to you but to everyone around you. While we cannot control what happened in the past, we do have the ability to heal emotional wounds, nurture the wounded inner child, and regain our sense of playfulness and optimism.

In the next chapter, we will learn more practices to help you connect with and heal your inner child.

Chapter 5: Inner Child Healing Practices

Healing journeys do not necessarily need to be long, drawn-out processes that require years of hard work. Healing and transformation always begin with learning and discovery—the magic that feeds the dynamic, powerful inner child within.

–Cary G. Weldy

Our emotions have a powerful influence on us. They can be triggered by anything at any time—from the places you visit to certain people you encounter—and can completely throw you off balance. If we want to experience pure bliss in life, we must find the courage to heal emotional pain. The healing process is different for everyone. But the one thing in common is that it is a continuous process that requires you to consistently keep reapplying certain techniques and practices in your life to help you manage your emotions.

In the previous chapter, we learned about the most common core beliefs that are a result of traumatic childhood experiences. Now, to move on to the healing process, you will need to revisit your journal and go over the core beliefs that you identified with in Chapter 4.

To address each core belief, write down the answers to the following questions:

- What childhood experiences made you feel this way (based on the core belief)?
- When did you develop this belief?
- Is there a person in particular who hurt you the most in the past? If so, who?
- What are the three most painful experiences from your childhood that come to your mind?

Reconnecting with and relating to your inner child is like any other connection. It requires patience and understanding for the relationship to grow. Digging up long-buried pain can be intimidating at first but letting go of emotional pain allows you to feel safe again.

Healing Your Past Experiences

Healing your inner child involves identifying the experiences that caused you pain and recognizing their impact on your life. It focuses on ensuring that your inner child feels the love, support, and safety it never experienced in your childhood. Working with your inner child allows you to reconcile a vital part of your being because your inner child controls your behaviors and the decisions you make in your career, relationships, and entire life. In order to change the negative behaviors that result from your unmet childhood needs, you must introduce your inner child to a new approach.

The practices we will learn in this chapter can be done at any time of the day; however, creating a routine can help you maintain consistency and integrate them with your existing daily habits to achieve effective results. You can do the exercises at the beginning of the day, in the evening right before bedtime, or when you are triggered and feel upset or overwhelmed. As you learn to identify your inner child through certain behaviors, try doing the exercises when feelings of sadness, anger, anxiety, or disappointment surface.

The more you practice inner child healing, the easier it will be to recognize your emotional wounds and how they manifest themselves. Remember, you do not have to go through the healing process alone. If the wounds are extremely overwhelming, you can seek the help of a therapist to guide you through the process.

Ways to Heal Your Inner Child

Journal as Your Inner Child

Journaling is an excellent way to reflect on your thoughts, feelings, and emotions. It can help you recognize the behavior patterns you developed as a child that are getting in the way of living a happier, fulfilled life. To practice effective journaling, set your adult self aside and journal as your younger self. You can use a photograph of yourself as a child or visualize your child self at the specific age you want to explore.

Exercise:

1. Only start doing the following exercises if you feel that you can handle them emotionally. Remember that there are a lot of therapists that can help you if you feel that you cannot go through an experience alone. If

you are ready, close your eyes and imagine a specific traumatizing event.

2. Next, identify the form of neglect you experienced and write it down–often trauma goes hand in hand with some form of neglect—a lack of love, security, or autonomy. Knowing the form of neglect can help you to identify what areas you need to focus on to make your inner child feel comfortable and safe every day.

3. Feel the emotions that come up during the exercise. Feeling your emotions is extremely important. It allows you to let go of your painful experiences and negative beliefs.

4. Next, visualize yourself having a dialogue with your caregiver or the person who caused you pain in the past. You can say something like, "I know you're trying your best to show that you love me, but this is not an appropriate way of doing it."

5. Then, listen to your inner child—listen to what he or she wanted to hear. For example, did he or she want to be hugged and told that everything is going to be okay? Did your younger self want to hear the words "You are enough," "What happened is not your fault," or "You acknowledge that he or she tried

their best?" If it is difficult to listen to your younger child, you can also imagine that the experience happened to another child. Do what you would intuitively do as an adult in this situation. Often it is exactly what you need.

6. Be present and stay in this moment until you feel that your inner child feels safe and happy again. Repeat the exercise with other experiences.

7. Repeat the exercise for the same experience multiple times. It is not enough to do this exercise once. With my most painful experiences, I had to repeat them often to finally let go and heal myself.

Allow yourself to feel the emotions that come up during your journaling exercise. When I first began practicing the inner child healing concept, I always tried to do the exercise without feeling the emotions because I was afraid of the ones that might come up. Allowing yourself to feel your emotions can feel overwhelming at first, but it is important in your healing process. For example, if you have a splinter in your finger, it is not enough to disinfect the wound and put a plaster over it. Sometimes you have to laboriously pull the splinter out of your skin. It may bleed, but later the wound will heal, and you will feel relieved.

Some common emotions that may come up during the exercise include feelings of fear and grief for the love that you were seeking so hard but never received. You may feel the pain of not being good enough, or you may feel angry because of all the things you never had that you wanted. It is normal to feel this way. Try not to suppress these feelings and instead experience them. This will help you let go of them and free yourself from past pain.

Write a Letter to Your Inner Child

Acknowledging your inner child is an important step toward connecting with yourself. If you met your six-year-old self today, what would you say to him or her? Perhaps you would like to apologize to him for the things that happened and let him know that everything is going to be okay. Or, maybe you would like to tell her how beautiful she is. Whatever it may be that will make your inner child feel safe and protected, writing a letter to your younger self can help you deeply connect with yourself.

Writing a letter to your inner child brings the events of the past into present-day light so you can identify what issues need to be resolved. It is confronting your fears and limitations and forgiving the things that still hold you back from living a courageous life. It is a way to soften your hardened heart and open it up so you can let love freely flow in and out of the long-forgotten chambers of your delicate soul.

Writing a letter to your younger self brings all the separated pieces of yourself together so you can feel whole again. It allows you to tell your inner child what he or she longs to hear—and give them the love, affection, and reassurance they need.

When writing your letter, you can write about your childhood memories from an adult perspective and explain why certain things happened that you could not understand as a child. For example, if you never understood why your mother spent less time at home with you. You could explain that it was because she had to work just so you could have all the things you needed and a better future.

When writing your letter, keep the following ideas in mind:

- Your body remembers all your traumatic experiences even if you try to suppress your feelings. So, be honest when writing your letter, and take time to listen to the unspoken desires of your wounded inner child.

- By writing this letter, you are finally listening to your own needs.

- Through this letter, you are allowing yourself to let go of the fear of judgment and giving yourself permission to feel your emotions.
- When you finish writing the letter, take some time to read it like it is yours because it is.

Exercise:

1. Find a quiet place where you feel safe and can be open and vulnerable.
2. Imagine yourself sitting in a beautiful garden, filled with colorful flowers, and all you can hear is the distant sound of birds chirping. Feel the cool air breeze gently brush your cheeks.
3. Take in the beauty of this place and feel the peacefulness that comes with being in this serene place.
4. Now, while sitting there, imagine your six-year-old self coming to sit next to you.
5. Ask yourself, what you'd like to tell your younger self. What did your six-year-old self want to hear that they were never told? What did he or she want to know? If you could validate and affirm your younger self, what would you say to them?

6. Then, ask your inner child the following questions:

    a. How do you feel?

    b. What can I do to make you feel better?

    c. How can I support you more?

7. Take a few deep breaths in, and feel this experience. Take note of all the memories that come up.

You may find that you experienced trauma at different stages in your life, not just in early childhood. Perhaps there was an event that happened in your adolescent years that caused you pain. You can use the same exercise to visualize yourself at that age.

Sorting through painful past experiences is not an easy thing to do. But, when you open yourself up to doing the work needed to heal, you will realize this is just what your inner child needs.

Affirm Your Inner Child

When you affirm your inner child, you meet an emotional need that was not met when you were young. You are embracing and empowering your inner child and allowing them to feel heard and seen. One of the many ways to affirm your inner child is by imagining yourself as a child, surrounded by all the people you love and want to love, embrace, and understand you. The following exercise will help you connect and reframe your beliefs about your self-worth.

Exercise:

1. Find a quiet place where you can sit in silence.

2. Close your eyes and imagine loving people from your childhood. It could be your parents, friends, grandparents, or neighbors. If you do not remember loving people from your childhood, imagine having loving parents, the way you would have loved your parents to ideally be.

3. Then, imagine your younger self. If you have difficulty seeing a clear picture of yourself as a child, I highly suggest looking at old photos of yourself.

4. Imagine yourself having a dialogue with those loving people. Hear them tell you "I love you," "I am so happy that you are here," "I am so proud of you," "I am always here for you,"and "I will always keep you safe."

Let Go of the Past

A lot of people feel angry about what happened in the past, and this is normal when you have suffered trauma. The traumatic experiences you went through and the way certain people—whom you trusted—treated you were unfair. For the longest time, you may have subconsciously believed that you were at fault, even though you were just a child and had no experience to handle the situation. It is okay to be angry, sad, anxious, and all the other emotions that may come up; however, it is also important to move onto a brighter future.

Acknowledge and accept that what happened in the past is part of your story. Find ways to move forward to a brighter future. Healing takes time and patience. It will not happen overnight, but with time, you will start to feel better about yourself.

The following exercise helped me to let go of emotional pain, and I hope that as you do these exercises, you will be able to find peace and the ability to let go of past hurts.

Ways to Help You Let Go of the Past

1. Write down one of your painful experiences. Ensure that you use "I accept" in your response to how you felt about the experience. For example, "I accept to have felt lonely" or

"I accept that people were unfair to me". Repeat this to yourself whenever you feel that your past is too dominant in your life. This will help you acknowledge your feelings.

2. Practice forgiveness—Forgiving can be a powerful tool to help you let go of the past. By forgiving yourself, your experiences, and the people who hurt you, you liberate yourself from the prison of past emotional wounds and find ways to move forward with your life. In my journey, this helped me a lot to empathize with the persons that were unfair to me and think about their wounds, their backgrounds, and life experience. However, forgiving the past is a personal choice and you don't have to forgive to heal your inner child. Whether you decide to forgive or not, this is a decision you have to make yourself. The purpose of inner child healing is not about forgiving or not forgiving your past experiences, it is about your personal journey of self-discovery and coming home to yourself.

3. Practice mindfulness—Mindfulness allows you to connect to the present and not remain in the past. It allows you to focus your

thoughts and attention on your current emotions and environment and, therefore reduces stress and thoughts about the past.

4. Practice meditation—I highly recommend meditation to help you release past pain and tension from your body. Meditation is a powerful tool for healing and managing stress. It has a lot of physical, emotional, and psychological benefits and allows you to gain a new perspective on what happened in the past.

I have noticed that some people are afraid of sitting in silence with their own thoughts. Some even say meditation feels weird; however, meditating does not have to be done while sitting with your legs crossed and eyes closed while chanting a mantra. You can practice meditation anywhere and at any time. For instance, the next time you wash your dishes, try focusing your attention on the present moment and observing yourself. Feel the sensation of the water touching your skin as you rinse the dishes. Pay attention to how you feel—feel the peace and calm within your body.

Recreate Your Belief System Through Positive Affirmations

Words that were spoken to you by your peers and family, or the physical trauma you experienced shaped your belief system. Beliefs make it difficult for you to tell the difference between who you think you are and your authentic self. This is because many times we hide our true selves behind the beliefs we have developed over the years.

Now that you understand how beliefs impact your behavior, it is time to replace those harmful, negative beliefs with new, empowering ones that will make your inner child feel respected, loved, and cared for. The following ideas can help you reframe your beliefs.

Identify Your Negative Core Beliefs

Revisit the core beliefs you identified in Chapter 4 under "Uncovering Your Beliefs."

Recognize That it is Just a Belief

Recognize that your beliefs are nothing more than simply statements that are not backed by facts.

Reframe Your Beliefs

Against each belief, write the opposite of that belief. For example, if the core belief is "I am not allowed to express my feelings." Replace it with" I am allowed to express my feelings."

Another way to use positive affirmations is to record them on a recording device such as your phone or tablet and listen to them while driving to work, taking a walk, or during a guided meditation. You can also post notes around the house—on your fridge, in your bedroom, or on your bathroom mirror—and say them out loud while looking yourself in the eyes.

Challenge Your Beliefs

Ask yourself if the belief is grounded and supported by facts. To help you reframe your beliefs, ask yourself the following challenging questions:

- Reality testing:
    - Is there evidence to back up your beliefs?
    - Are your thoughts backed by evidence or are they just your perceptions?

- Is there a way to find out if these thoughts are true?

- Find alternative reasons:
    - What else do your thoughts mean?
    - If you reframe your thoughts to positive ones, how would you view the situation?
    - Is there another way you can perceive the situation?
    - If you had a different belief what would it be and how would it change your life?
- Put things into perspective:
    - Are your beliefs helping you live a fulfilled life?
    - What is the worst-case scenario? What are the chances the worst can happen?
    - Is the situation as terrible as you make it out to be?

Recognize the Damaging Effects Caused by Negative Beliefs

Are your beliefs allowing you to make objective decisions in your life, or do you base your decisions on past experiences? Recognize the damaging effects your beliefs have on your success. Identify how your negative beliefs have held you back in the past. For example, it could delay you from making a decision about a job offer because of the fear of past failure until the offer is given to someone else.

Observe Your Thoughts

Often, we are unaware of our thoughts and, therefore, do not recognize when the negative ones creep in. Most of the time, we operate from the subconscious, which makes it difficult to spot negative thoughts.

Paying attention to your thoughts can help you identify them when your mind starts running out of control. Keep a journal with you always if you can and write down your thoughts each time you feel overwhelmed. Keeping track of your thoughts will help you spot repeating patterns and find effective ways to reframe your thinking.

Implementing these strategies will help you reframe your negative beliefs and allow you to form new, positive ones that align with who you want to be.

It is important to note that there is no age limit to developing a new mindset and way of thinking. You can reframe your beliefs no matter your age. Challenging your beliefs can help you gain a new perspective on them and your current situation. It can raise your awareness of how negative beliefs hold you back more than they help you progress in life. The most effective way to get positive results when developing new habits is to practice them consistently. I had to consistently practice reframing my beliefs over the past couple of years in order to see positive change. The more I practiced these exercises, the more I became aware of my triggers and the emotional pain that lay in the deepest parts of my being. I uncovered painful experiences from my past and learned that the only way to deal with emotional pain is to bring it to the surface and not bury it inside of you.

At the beginning of your healing journey, you may feel like you are not doing it the right way. Sometimes, you may feel like there is no change, but remember, nothing is easy when you first start out. Give your healing process time. Understanding your inner child takes time and patience and may seem daunting because you are still getting to know your inner child. However, the more you connect with your inner child, the better you will understand yourself. It is important to be patient and consistent throughout your healing process. It took years to develop your beliefs; therefore, healing will not happen overnight. If you have not cleaned your house in over thirty years, you cannot expect to clean it once and expect it to be completely clean. It will take a bit more time and effort to dust off and polish all surfaces and to have a squeaky clean house.

While practicing these exercises, keep the following ideas in mind:

- Healing starts when you acknowledge that your inner child exists.
- Working with your inner child allows you to reconcile an important part of your being that is responsible for the decisions you make in life.
- Some of the most effective ways to heal your inner child include:
    - Journaling—writing down your thoughts can help you spot negative thoughts and can help you identify repeating patterns.

    - Write a letter to your inner child—in the process of learning to cope with emotional pain, you may have suppressed your feelings. Writing a letter to your younger self is another way to affirm your inner child.
    - The only way to release emotional pain is to let go of it. Holding on to past experiences does more damage to your physical, emotional, and mental well-being than good.
    - Reframe your beliefs—reframing your beliefs means conditioning yourself through a new belief system and creating the reality you want to see in your life.
- To change your negative beliefs, you have got to challenge your thoughts. Are your beliefs about yourself backed by facts or are they just your own perceptions?
- Recognize the effects that negative beliefs have on your life. When you realize the opportunities you have missed because of fear of reliving the past, you will find the inspiration to change your beliefs.

- Learn to be present and observe your thoughts. Keeping track of your thoughts will help you identify your triggers and allow you to find ways to reframe your thinking.

- Healing is a lifelong journey and you do not achieve results by practicing these exercises once. It takes time and consistent effort to change the beliefs you developed over the past decades.

In the next chapter, we will learn how to manage your triggers through self-care and self-love practices. If you struggle with setting boundaries, we will explore ways in which you can set and reinforce healthy boundaries in your life.

Chapter 6: Managing Trauma Triggers

Let us listen to the needs of our inner child which is being tamed and imprisoned by the rules of a grown-up world. –Erik Pevernagie

You may have experienced how the past can have a hold over you at some point in your life. Perhaps it is the scent of a particular perfume that transports you down memory lane to a specific time and place that reminds you of the day you met your first love. Or, maybe it is a restaurant where you had Sunday lunch every weekend with your parents growing up. While happy thoughts are often worth remembering and remind us of the good times we have had with people we love, there are times when intrusive, negative thoughts invade our minds. The thoughts of the painful experiences we went through growing up can appear all of a sudden without notice and disrupt the way you function.

Negative thoughts can suck you back into the traumatic experience you went through and cause the same physical and emotional response as the one you experienced in the past. It almost feels like you are reliving that moment.

Before we delve deep into understanding how triggers affect you, let us define what a trigger is. A trigger is anything that reminds you of a past traumatic experience. Remember the story I shared earlier about how I would throw my books on the floor while studying because of my frustration? I was often triggered by the belief that I was not good enough. Triggers can be anything—a thought, a place, a person, or even something as small as not knowing how to solve a specific school exercise. The experience triggers a lot of past beliefs and can cause us to react disproportionately.

Triggers often make you feel unsafe, fearful, helpless, and extremely emotional, and sometimes you may experience flashbacks. In other words, you feel the same emotions you felt when you first went through the experience, and your reaction to the trigger is a way to protect yourself from the perceived threat.

The severity of the reaction to a trigger depends on the person but, often, it takes a while for the nervous system to recover from the shock. Trauma creates an imbalance in your emotional state of being and reduces your ability to think clearly and act rationally. This raises your stress levels and can make you feel emotionally overwhelmed.

Type of Triggers

Triggers can be internal—caused by stress, sadness, or anger—or external—caused by environmental factors.

Internal Triggers

These include:

- pain
- anger and frustration
- anxiety
- feeling lonely and abandoned
- feeling out of control
- tension.

External Triggers

These include:

- arguments
- end of a relationship

- scents
- holidays and anniversaries
- places
- people
- witnessing tragedy
- movies, songs, and books

How to Manage Childhood Trauma Triggers

Healing emotional trauma can be overwhelming, and sometimes ignoring it may seem like an easy way out of pain. However, avoiding doing the work is not an effective solution. It prevents you from grabbing opportunities when they present themselves and creates unnecessary fear and anxiety. It is healthier to identify your triggers and find ways to manage them than to avoid them. With time and consistent practice, you will learn to manage and gain more control of your reactions.

Like any other healing process, the first step to managing childhood trauma triggers is to realize when your inner child takes over. For instance, when you start experiencing signs such as feelings of unworthiness, being dissatisfied with your physical appearance, or feeling fearful, anxious, and depressed. Another way to detect when your inner child takes over is if you are able to show empathy to others because, like a child, your inner child is more egocentric than your adult self.

Being triggered is a very vulnerable moment. Sometimes you may not immediately know what is triggering you at that particular moment. So, in order to think clearly and act rationally, first try to:

1. Take a deep breath.

2. Create distance between you and the trigger for a moment. For example, if you are talking to someone, put your phone away, end the conversation, and tell the other person in a neutral way that you need space to think for a moment.

The following ideas will help calm you down and allow you to think and react rationally to the situation.

Be Aware of What Is Happening

If it is possible to always have your notebook or journal with you. Keep it close to you—you will need it most of the time. When you feel a trigger response, call it out or write down in your journal:

- How is your body reacting?
- What thoughts are coming up in your mind?
- What is your emotional response?
- Is the trigger caused by feelings of stress or by your environment?

Being aware of your triggers can help you identify patterns that repeat so you can change your future responses.

Allow Yourself to Feel Your Emotions

We experience a lot of suffering because we do not allow ourselves to feel our emotions and we suppress our feelings. Allow yourself to feel the negative emotions that come along with triggers without judgment. Acknowledge and embrace them. Often, when we accept negative emotions, they slowly begin to dissipate because we are not rejecting them but acknowledging that they are there and not allowing them to influence our actions. A good example is that of a child. Children are naturally not afraid of expressing their feelings. They cry in public without shame, and when they suddenly see a horse, a bird, or something that excites them, they are suddenly happy again. They feel their emotions and can easily release them. Unfortunately, most of us grow up in societies where we are told to reject certain emotions and be ashamed to express them. We are taught to suppress our emotions and told not to cry, although emotions are important in teaching us to pay attention to our needs.

Practice Mindfulness

Mindfulness is the ability to focus on the present moment. Being mindful can help you be more aware of your thoughts, feelings, emotions, and environment. Triggers can pull you right into your past if you are not grounded and self-aware.

Mindfulness techniques such as listening to soothing music, taking deep breaths, taking a walk in nature, or inhaling a relaxing scent you can take your mind out of the dark experience and bring it back into the light of the present moment. Being present can help you realize that a trigger is not the actual experience of trauma but an after-effect of past events, and this can help calm you down.

Practice Self-Compassion

Often, when you experience a trigger, it is difficult to show compassion for yourself and for others. Sometimes we are harsh on ourselves and react irrationally toward certain situations. If you have been criticizing yourself for a long time, it can prove difficult to suddenly be compassionate toward yourself. Your feelings and emotions are valid, allow yourself to feel them and acknowledge them, no matter how small the trigger response may seem.

When you feel triggered, ask yourself what triggered your response—is it a lack of autonomy, a lack of attention, or feelings of loneliness? Take some time to reflect and talk to your inner child. You can say something like, "It is okay; I understand you." This way, you learn to validate your feelings instead of avoiding them. Then give your inner child the love and attention he or she longs for.

During my university days, when I felt stressed out and overwhelmed, I often got up and went into the bathroom. I already knew that the source of my frustration was the negative belief I had that "I was not good enough."

I would walk into the bathroom, stand in front of the mirror, and say to myself, "Milena, you have got this! It only seems difficult right now, but you are extremely smart and you can do this. Let us take a walk in nature—it will help you clear your mind and re-energize you." This simple practice gave me time to reflect on my thoughts and my feelings and often gave me a new perspective on my work and how I could approach my assignments differently. From this experience, I learned to separate my identity from my outcomes.

To help you practice self-compassion, ask yourself the following questions

- How can I be more compassionate right now?
- Is there a way I can distance myself from what is triggering me?
- What can I do to make myself feel better?

As you go through your healing journey, remember to be kind to yourself. You have been through a lot—emotionally and psychologically. The process of healing emotional trauma takes time; therefore, try and be more compassionate with yourself and the people around you. Pay attention to your needs and the things that help reduce stress. Make it a priority to take care of your mental health.

Practice Self-Love and Self-Care

When you experience emotional neglect, a lack of trust, love, attention, and isolation, it is normal to have a negative perception of people. If you felt unsafe and unloved in the past, it is important to build and nurture loving relationships in adulthood where you feel safe and supported.

Learn to prioritize yourself and your needs. I know it can be difficult at first if you have spent most of your time putting everyone's needs ahead of yours. Give yourself what you need—acceptance, validation, love, attention, safety—whatever it is you lacked as a child. You will notice a change in the way you feel and behave as your inner child starts to feel heard and seen.

Exercise:

Take an old photo album and old pictures of yourself. If you have recorded videos, that will work as well. It is in our nature to feel love and compassion when we see children. Looking at your childhood photos can help you generate feelings of love and compassion.

When you feel frustrated and are hard on yourself, try the following exercise:

- Treat yourself as you would your own child in this manner.
- Take a break from social media.
- Take a day off from work and create time for yourself.
- Go to bed early and get eight hours of sleep.
- Ask yourself what you need right now.
- Create work-life balance.
- Eat healthier.
- Exercise more.

Practicing this exercise will help you prioritize yourself more. Each time you feel triggered, ask your inner child, "How can I be more supportive of you", or, "What do you need from me today?" Acknowledging your inner child will make you feel safe.

Set Healthy Boundaries

When people hear the term "setting boundaries," they often think about something like a wall to keep everyone out. While keeping certain people out of your life can be beneficial to your mental well-being, it is not the only solution to creating peace and harmony in your life.

Setting healthy boundaries is vital to protecting your emotional and mental well-being. In this context, boundaries are not solid lines you draw on the ground to let people see how close they can get to you. Instead, they are limits you set around your body, emotions, mental well-being, and time to help preserve your energy and protect your overall well-being. Setting boundaries will help you avoid the stress and frustration of having your limits violated. Boundaries can also prevent people from manipulating you, especially if you are a yes-person and struggle to say no to others.

Boundaries communicate how you want to be treated and the things you cannot tolerate. Often, we are afraid of communicating our boundaries for fear of hurting people or losing love and approval from others. But if you communicate your boundaries in a compassionate way, often people will understand and respect them.

Types of Boundaries

There are different types of boundaries you can set for yourself, depending on your circumstances. You can set boundaries around your personal time and space, emotional energy, intellect, finances, or sexuality. You can set boundaries with your family, coworkers, strangers, intimate partner, and friends. Here are the seven boundaries that you need:

- Physical boundaries—these are limits you set around your body and physical space.
    - For example, the distance you are comfortable with when someone sits next to you or what you allow into your house.
- Time boundaries—these are limits you set on how you spend your time as well as who you spend it with.
    - For example, not taking work-related phone calls in the evenings so you can spend time with your family.
- Emotional and mental boundaries—these are limits that protect your thoughts and feelings so you are accountable for your feelings and do not have people undermine and invalidate them.
    - For example, not being comfortable sharing certain details of your personal life.
- Sexual boundaries—these are limits to what you choose to do or not do with your intimate partner including what you decide to share about your sexual history. You can also set sexual limits to the kind of intimacy you

want to have, where you want to have it, and with whom.
    - For example, you can set boundaries in how you want to be touched during intimacy.
- Financial boundaries—these are limits you set to protect your finances and assets.
    - For example, the amount of money you are comfortable loaning someone and who you are comfortable loaning it to.
- Spiritual boundaries—these are limits you set to protect your spiritual or religious beliefs.
    - For example, setting aside specific times of the day for your spiritual practices.
- Non-negotiable boundaries—these are limits you set to protect your sense of security and are non-negotiable.
    - Not suffering from physical or psychological violence.

How to Set Healthy Boundaries

When setting boundaries, it is important to remember that you are not responsible for other people's feelings, and therefore, you do not need to justify yourself. Be compassionate toward others, but remember to put yourself and your needs first. This is not selfishness, as some people may call it, but self-love.

I am a huge empath. Setting and respecting my own boundaries is the most difficult thing I have had to learn to do. I always found myself putting myself in the other person's shoes and thinking, "This person would be hurt"—just like a typical empath would predict how other people feel.

Setting boundaries allows you to put yourself first instead of always putting other people's needs ahead of yours. The following ideas will help you communicate your limits in a clear manner that people will understand.

1. Identify when you need to set boundaries—to set healthy boundaries, first have a clear understanding of what is happening.
    a. Do you feel uncomfortable, emotional, or depleted?
2. Set boundaries earlier on in your relationships—this can be difficult to do in already existing relationships but is quite helpful in letting everyone know where they stand to avoid confusion and frustration.
3. Communicate your boundaries across—let people know your limits and do not assume

that just because you respect their boundaries they must know to respect yours. Clearly communicating how you want to be treated can prevent conflicts and misunderstandings in your relationships. To communicate your boundaries without being aggressive:

a. Stay calm—your message will be received with less resistance when you remain calm.

b. Be specific and explain what you need, for how long, and what you expect from the other person.

c. Use "I" statements—for example, instead of saying" I need some space," try "I want to use the next two hours for me and go for a walk, and I would like to not be contacted until I come back."

4. Learn to say, "No"—it is not selfishness but simply understanding and meeting your own needs. If you cannot go out on Friday evening with your coworkers because you are working on a personal project, try to not look for excuses because you do not need an excuse to say no. Instead, you can show your gratitude. For example, "Thank you for inviting me but I am not available this Friday."

5. Be consistent with your boundaries—letting your limits slide can lead to confusion and violation of them. Consistently reinforcing your boundaries will ensure that they remain clear to people.

There is no need to be afraid to set boundaries in your life. Genuine friends will never abandon you because you said "No" to them. Practice self-compassion always, and you will realize that your needs matter and your feelings are valid. Setting healthy boundaries allows you to meet your inner child's needs and make him or her feel safe and protected. The more you meet your emotional needs, the better you will feel about yourself.

The following exercise will help you hold yourself accountable for setting and reinforcing boundaries and meeting your emotional needs.

Exercise:

- Write a letter to yourself.
- In the letter, make the following promises to your inner child:
    - You are going to take better care of him or her.
    - You are not going to criticize yourself anymore.

    - You are going to be more compassionate to yourself.
    - You will set and reinforce boundaries to protect him or her.
    - You will listen to his or her needs.

When triggers are not managed, they can affect your psychological and physical well-being. Remember, if working on your own to overcome triggers feels overwhelming, you do not have to do it alone. Working with a therapist can help you find effective ways to manage your triggers. While learning to identify childhood trauma triggers, keep the following in mind:

- A trigger is anything that reminds you of a past traumatic experience.
- A trigger can be a person, place, specific scent, object, or sound. They can be internal or external.
- The first step to managing a trigger is to identify when you are triggered.
    - Do you feel anxious, angry, or afraid?
- Be aware of what is happening around you that could be triggering you.
    - Is it the environment you are in?

    - Is it the person you are with?
    - Or, is it a negative thought that came to your mind?

- Practice mindfulness when you feel triggered. It will help you be more aware of your thoughts, feelings, and environment.

- Be compassionate to yourself and the people around you. You have been through trauma. Allow yourself to heal, and keep in mind that healing is a process that takes time.

- Learn to put your needs first. Practicing self-love and self-care allows you to meet your emotional needs.

- Learn to set and reinforce boundaries. Communicating your boundaries lets people know exactly how you want to be treated and can help you avoid the stress that results from people stepping over your boundaries.

In the next chapter, we will learn how to reconnect with your healed inner child and find ways to inspire your creativity and reawaken your curiosity.

Chapter 7: Reconnecting With Your Healed Inner Child

We nurture our creativity when we release our inner child. Let it run and roam free. It will take you on a brighter journey. –Serina Hartwell

When was the last time you had fun and did something that ignited your soul? Imagine for a second—if you had the confidence and ability to pursue the life you desired, what would you do? What career would you pursue? What kind of relationships would you build? Would you still live in fear, or would you live boldly each day knowing that life is full of endless possibilities and adventures and that you have skills that you can use to bring change into the world?

If you knew that you were born with a creative side and have the ability to use your imagination to connect to that part of you that knows no boundaries. The part of you that has been buried under piles of emotional wounds—that only your inner child knows. Would life be any different for you?

If you realized that you were born with natural gifts and talents, and that you are not as hopeless as some people made you believe, how would you use your gifts and talents?

Most people have believed for so long that they are not good enough that it has become their reality. We have normalized covering up emotional pain and shoving it deep within ourselves, such that it has become the source of most of our problems. We have gotten so used to dealing with the challenges of adulthood that we have forgotten how to truly connect with our playful side.

Reconnecting with your healed inner child allows you to let go of the cares of this world, and appreciate the beauty of each moment that passes by. It teaches you to express yourself without fear of judgment. When you start working with your inner child you allow yourself to explore new possibilities, and reconnect with your creative side. You get to know your authentic self–without the negative, self-limiting beliefs.

What it Means to Reconnect With Your Inner Child

Inner child healing connects you to the positive aspects of your childlike nature. We are all born with a sense of curiosity, zest, and optimism, and we have the ability to develop empathy, compassion, resilience, and self-reliance. Reconnecting with your inner child allows you to see yourself beyond what others think of you. It allows you to be who you truly are—to come back home to yourself.

How Reconnecting With Your Inner Child Can Change Your Life

It Renews Your Faith In People

Reconnecting with your inner child renews your faith in people and changes your worldview. You begin to notice the beauty in this world and accept people's differences in ideas, thoughts, and opinions. Slowly, you begin to trust again.

Children trust others naturally, which makes a true connection with other people quite easy. A child only stops trusting and believing in people when they are betrayed and their sense of security is threatened. Reconnecting with your inner child enables you to see the world in a different light.

It Sparks Your Creativity

When we hear the word "creativity," we often think of an artistic person. Pictures that usually come to mind are those of someone painting a portrait or of a poet expressing themself through rhythmic sounds that awaken your imaginative awareness. However, creativity is not for the select few individuals who have found purpose in using their natural gifts and talents. We all have a creative side that is unique to each of us. Just like intelligence, your creativity can grow with time and practice.

If you struggle with codependency, developing your creative side can teach you how to be an independent thinker and to believe in your own ideas. Creativity is crucial to your growth. It leads to a happier and more successful life.

It Ignites Curiosity

The urge to learn and acquire knowledge helps us grow in knowledge and experience. We live in a world that is constantly evolving and it is logical for us to grow along with it. We can learn so much about curiosity from children.

Children are honest and not afraid of anything. They learn about their environment by fearlessly pursuing objects and places that spark their curiosity. Leave a child in the living room with a piece of pottery on the coffee table; the child's first instinct would be to explore this fascinating object that has caught his or her attention.

A child will not talk themselves out of learning about their object of interest; instead, they will walk up to it unafraid, and only learn that they are not supposed to play with an expensive piece of art when an adult suddenly walks into the room and yells, "Do not touch that." Even when they are reprimanded, children will not stop learning about their environment—they are unafraid of rejection. A child only loses the power of their imagination when society tells them to be realistic. Only then do they stop believing in their ideas and in themselves.

Exercise

Take some time to go to the park or any place where children love to play. Sit and observe their every move.

- Watch how they play together and take turns on the swing or slide.
- Observe how they work together to build sand castles.
- Observe how they imitate each other and work harmoniously and do not compete with each other.

Spending time with children can help you tap into your playful side. I used to take care of my little cousin. Sometimes we would take walks in nature together, and I would watch in total awe at how he would stop every two steps just to look at a flower that caught his attention. This simple practice, which was unintentional, ended up being one of the greatest and most effective exercises that taught me to stay in the moment and be more mindful.

Ways to Reconnect With Your Inner Child

To help you connect with your inner child, the following practices can be a good place to start.

Recall Positive Childhood Memories

Take some time to think about some of the beautiful memories from your childhood. It could be a time when you visited the museum for the first time, your favorite school activities, or the games you played in your dollhouse with your friends. It could be anything that made you feel happy and always uplifted your spirit. Write down those memories in your journal.

If you cannot recall any beautiful memories, here are a few journaling prompts you can use to help you remember specific details of your childhood:

- What were the things you loved learning about?
- What were your favorite activities?
    - Why did you stop doing those activities?
    - Are you still interested in those activities?
    - If not, why?
- What places did you enjoy visiting?
- Where did you feel safest as a child?

- Who were your childhood friends?
- Why did you choose those friends to hang around with?
- What kind of books or films did you enjoy reading? And, why?
- What fascinated you the most as a child?
- Where and who did you spend your most enjoyable moments with?
- How did your dream life look as a child?
- What was your dream job?

Play

Adult responsibilities such as a career and family roles often take up much of our time, and we end up forgetting what it feels like to let loose and connect with our playful side. Sometimes you need to take life less seriously. What did you enjoy most doing when you were a child? Take time off and do those activities that excited you growing up.

Growing up, I used to love being out in nature—the fresh air, bright sun, and soft wind gently brushing my hair and cheeks. Everything around me seemed so huge—all the mountains and tall trees—but, somehow, I felt like I was a part of this huge universe. I felt like I belonged, and there was nothing to think about except experiencing Mother Nature's soft embrace.

I still sometimes drive to the nearest mountain from where I live and just sit there and connect with my inner child. This experience always takes me back to the times when I was happier and carefree. Listening to my favorite childhood music always reminds me that that happy and optimistic child still exists in me. Sometimes, I pack a picnic basket with all my favorite delicacies and just sit there and listen to the serene sounds of nature. It is such an amazing experience to let go of all your worries and allow yourself to be grounded and connected to nature. Carve out time in your busy schedule to have some fun. When you approach life lightheartedly, life becomes exciting and fun.

Express Yourself Openly

As adults, we are afraid to fully express our authentic selves. We have grown used to letting societal norms determine how we should behave. We are afraid that if we act differently from what is deemed normal behavior by others, we may appear as being weird. We become afraid to express our ideas for fear of rejection. Children are not afraid of being heard. They tell the truth as it is, which makes them authentic.

Expressing yourself allows people to see who you truly are. When you are unafraid to let people see the real you, only then can you build genuine relationships.

Reconnect with your inner child and learn to be honest and open about who you are and how you feel. Some people may not necessarily agree with your ideas; however, when you are genuine, you attract genuine people who love you for who you are.

Practice Meditation

Meditation is one of the most effective tools to build self-awareness and achieve inner peace. It teaches you to pay attention to your feelings and emotions and to acknowledge the uncomfortable emotions that come up in your life. When you learn to acknowledge your emotions, you learn to find healthy ways to express them. This can help validate your inner child and let them know that it is okay to express emotions.

Try this meditation exercise to reconnect, love, and acknowledge your inner child:

- Find a quiet place where you can sit or lie down comfortably, and not be interrupted.
- Gently close your eyes, and bring your attention to your breath.
- Allow your shoulders to soften, and follow the rhythm of your breathing.
- Relax your body muscles and think about the happiest moment from your childhood.
- Allow yourself to connect to that moment when your inner child felt safe, loved, and protected.
- If negative emotions show up, simply acknowledge them and be compassionate to your inner child for the pain they suffered.
- Then, gently, bring your mind back to the time when you felt safe as a child.
- Feel the immense feelings of joy and zeal for the life you felt.
- Acknowledge that a happy, innocent, cheerful, healthy child still exists in you.
- Recognize that your desire is for your inner child to feel loved, happy, and fulfilled; therefore, do everything to meet their needs.

- Then, picture your inner child smiling, happy, and carefree because you have met their needs.
- Stay in this moment, look deep into your inner child's eyes. Pay attention to how you feel as you connect to your healed inner child.
- In this moment, from within your heart, appreciate your inner child and send them love for their presence in your life.
- Now, imagine seeing yourself through the eyes of your inner child.
- Feel the love your inner child has for you. Stay in this moment, and feel that love grow within you.
- Immerse yourself in this moment and feel the wonderful feelings that come with meeting your inner child's needs.
- Now, rest in this new experience and pay attention to how you feel right now.

Remember, you are like a parent to your inner child. A good parent always wants what is best for their child and ensures that their child is well taken care of. A wise parent is there for their child every day, not just some days when they feel like it.

Healing your inner child is a process that requires you to be present every day.

Get Creative

One common trait all children have is the ability to use their imagination. Leave a child alone in a room, and they will not fail to find something to do that will keep them busy. If they do not have their toys next to them, they will use whatever is in front of them to play with. Children never run out of ideas.

When I started taking actual time to do the things I loved as a child, I did not have a lot of ideas about what to do exactly. At times, I would watch Disney movies and often found myself getting bored. I would go outside and play on the swing. I did all the stuff that children usually do that I could think of. However, I would still get bored.

I never gave up; instead, I would sit and ask myself, “What would ten-year-old me do next?” It was fascinating how new ideas would flow to me, and I would explore new ways to keep myself entertained that even as a child I never knew I enjoyed. As adults, we lose the ability to be bored. We are always distracted and always have something to do. If you are not thinking about your stressful job, you are worried about bills, how to keep your weight in check, or some other thing you need to do. Allowing yourself to get bored sometimes is important; it will help you generate more creative ideas.

Reconnecting with your inner child allows you to reconnect with your creative side. Children find joy and meaning in small pleasures. They enjoy painting, reading comic books, dancing, and singing. Take some time to get creative. Draw a painting, create a piece of art, go out somewhere serene and quiet, and let mother nature inspire your creativity.

Treat Yourself to Something Ridiculous

One of the biggest fears most people have is being seen as silly by others. We try so hard to adhere to societal norms about what we should do and not do. We worry more about what people would think if I ate a large slice of pizza than how it would make us feel. There is absolutely no shame in treating yourself to something you enjoy. Have that large ice cream cone, eat an enormous slice of pizza, or buy a stuffed animal toy to cuddle with every night. Do those ridiculous things that you loved as a child.

While working on connecting with your inner child, keep the following ideas in mind:

- Reconnecting with your inner child connects you to your creative and playful side that has been buried in layers of emotional pain.

- It allows you to see life through the eyes of your inner child.

- Healing your inner child renews your faith in people and changes the way you see the world.

- Children see opportunities all around them and do not get discouraged when they face challenges. Seeing life through the eyes of your inner child can reignite your creativity. It allows you to tap into your creative side and find creative solutions to some of your challenges.

- Reconnecting with your inner child ignites your curiosity. Children are curious, and curiosity and fearlessness allow them to learn about the world around them. When you are curious, you open yourself up to new knowledge and encourage your personal growth.

- Take some time to reflect on your childhood. Think of a time when you were happiest. It could be when you played in your dollhouse, or the time you visited the museum for the first time. Recalling positive memories from your childhood can help you reconnect with your healed inner child.

- Reconnecting with your inner child can help you tap into your playful side. Children love to play. They have the most fun when they play their favorite games. Carve out time in your busy life to have some fun.

- To reconnect with your inner child, learn to express yourself openly. Children are honest and unafraid to tell the truth. Being authentic means allowing people to see you for who you are. Do not be afraid to express your ideas and opinions because you fear losing people. When you are genuine, you attract genuine people and build healthy relationships.

- Meditation is one of the effective tools to help you connect with your inner child. It teaches you to accept your emotions—even the uncomfortable ones. When you learn to acknowledge your emotions, you can find healthy ways to express them.

- One of the many ways you can reconnect with your inner child is through your creativity. Children express themselves through their creativity. Whether it is through painting or coloring. Spend some time doing some art—paint a portrait of your favorite place or create a piece of pottery. It will help you tap into your creative side.

- Do not be afraid to treat yourself to something ridiculous. It is the smallest things that we often deem silly that bring us joy and fulfillment. So, treat yourself to a large ice cream or buy yourself a stuffed animal and sleep next to it every night. Whatever brings your inner child joy, do it because when your inner child is happy, you are happy.

It is normal to have questions about the inner child healing concept and its effectiveness in healing past trauma. Often, people wonder what to do when their partners and family members do not support their healing journey. In the next chapter, we will explore the answers to these questions you may have and help you gain more clarity on what to expect throughout your healing process.

Chapter 8: Frequently Asked Questions

Our wounds are often the openings into the best and most beautiful part of us. –David Richo

Doing inner child work is a process of rediscovering yourself. Through working with your inner child, you become more self-aware and self-conscious. The inner child concept teaches you to listen to yourself and pay attention to your feelings and emotions. It allows you to reconnect with your inner child and meet his or her unmet needs.

As you begin your healing journey, you may have questions about the concept and what to expect. People often wonder, "What happens if my partner does not want to practice inner child healing?" or, "My family is not supportive of my healing journey. What should I do?" You may even wonder how you would know if you were healing by practicing the concept. All these questions are important in helping you prepare for your healing journey. However, keep in mind that each inner child healing experience is unique to every individual. It is important to focus on the process rather than the results. This will allow you to treat your healing journey as a lifelong process and not a race to the finish line.

Throughout your lifetime, you will continue to go through different experiences and learn more about yourself and your inner child. When you reignite your curiosity and find new inspiration and zeal for life, you will find answers to most of the questions you may have. In this chapter, I have tried to answer a few of the common questions people ask me about inner child healing.

Common Questions About Inner Child Healing

Below are common questions people often ask about inner child healing.

What Parts of Life Are Affected by a Wounded Inner Child?

A wounded inner child affects all areas of your life. The negative beliefs you develop from childhood about yourself, other people, and the world in general impact your decisions. For example, if you believe that you are not good enough and are unworthy, you may live your life afraid to take risks and pursue new goals because you are afraid to fail.

Living in fear can cause you to miss out on career opportunities that may present themselves, which can improve your finances. It can prevent you from building healthy relationships because, deep down inside, you believe you are not worthy of genuine love.

The following are some of the common areas that are affected by negative beliefs that can hold you back from living a fulfilled life.

Relationships

Here are a few examples of negative beliefs that can affect your relationships:

- I am unworthy of love.
- I cannot trust my partner.
- I have to sacrifice my needs to receive love.
- I am only attracted to unavailable people.
- Men (or women) are the problem.
- Only lucky people find love.

- I will never find someone who understands me.
- No one likes me.
- I am afraid of being rejected.
- I am not attractive enough to receive love.

These negative beliefs can affect the way you perceive relationships and other people. It is not the right person that will make your relationship problems disappear, it is identifying the underlying cause of your beliefs and developing a strong desire for love.

Career

Do you find it difficult to make decisions and take risks in your career? Do opportunities for a better position that comes with a pay upgrade and more responsibilities scare you so much that you would rather stay in your current position? Do you struggle to say "No" to your coworkers and are known as the guy who is always willing to help others with their projects even when you have your own pile of work to deal with? If your work is sucking the joy out of your life, it may be time to reevaluate some of your beliefs about money and self-worth.

Negative beliefs about yourself can

- lead you to decline opportunities to grow in your career by avoiding applying for new roles often because you feel you are not good enough or qualified for the role.
- prevent you from taking risks and lead you to procrastinate because you lack self-confidence, which often leads to stagnation in your career.
- result in perfectionism and setting unrealistic goals, often because you attach your sense of worth to your results.
- make you a people-pleaser because you feel that for everyone to like you, you have to put their needs ahead of yours.
- lead to poor problem-solving skills because you avoid solving problems and conflicts for fear of not being loved in the workplace.

Common negative beliefs that can lead to stagnation in your career include:

- I am not qualified for this position.
- There are people better suited for this role than I am.

- My work is not perfect yet, so I have to put in more hours.
- I cannot say "No" to my colleagues; they would hate me.
- I am not talented enough.
- No one is supportive of me.
- I would rather stick to job security than pursue something else.

Finances

Negative beliefs about money often stem from our upbringing—from our family members, friends, and the society we grew up in, among other factors. A person who grew up in a home where financial resources were scarce and their parents struggled to get by is likely to believe that money is difficult to come by.

The following beliefs about money often develop as a result of our experiences:

- Money is hard to come by.
- There is not enough money to go around.
- I do not want a lot of money; I just want enough to get by.

- Having a lot of money is selfish.
- You need money to make money.
- You have to work hard to get wealthy.
- Money is a limited resource.
- In order to have a lot of money, you have to use and take advantage of people.
- You have to hold on to every dime you make.
- It is more enlightening to be poor than rich.
- Money cannot make you happy.
- Money is the root of evil.
- I am bad with my finances.

Money is not evil. If anything, having enough financial resources allows you to do good in this world.

If you are a philanthropist, financial resources can enable you to do a lot of good in this world, in your family, and in your community. Before I started working on changing my beliefs about money, I had the belief that rich people were bad people. Healing my inner child helped me realize that your motive is key to what you do when you have a lot of money. You can do a lot of bad things with money, but you can also do a lot of good to bring change to this world.

Your Body Image

Your beliefs about your body stem from the ideas of your family, friends, tradition, and the society you grew up in. These ideas shape how you see yourself. Negative body image is associated with:

- eating disorders
- low self-esteem
- mood disorders
- social anxiety
- depression
- relationship problems

Some of the common beliefs about body image include:

- There is something wrong with me.
- Nothing looks good on me.
- I hate the way I look.
- I wish my body looked like his or hers.
- I would be happier if I lost a bit of weight.

- I hate my (thighs, arms, legs, and so on).
- I am ugly.
- My skin is too dark.
- I would be happier if I had clear skin.

Negative beliefs can prevent you from living the life you desire. In the previous chapters, we talked about belief systems and how they affect different areas of your life. It is important that you look at each aspect of your life individually and assess your core beliefs in those areas and how they impact your life.

Is it Normal to Feel Anger Towards Your Parents?

Often, when people realize their parents' mistakes and how unfairly they were treated in the past, they tend to be angry and resent their parents. When someone discovers how a parent failed to love and protect them as well as stand up for them when they needed it the most, they become resentful—which may seem like a proper reaction to someone who betrayed your trust. However, it is not a healthy solution to deal with trauma.

Our parents made their mistakes, and when you think about why they did certain things, you may find that they did not know any better, so they did the best they could with whatever little information they had.

Anger can be an important step toward healing. It is normal to experience feelings of anger towards the person who caused you pain, and often, this is an important step in the healing process. It allows you to stop blaming yourself for other people's mistakes that you were not responsible for. However, it is not healthy to remain angry forever. If not addressed, anger can consume you and infiltrate every area of your life. It destroys your faith in people—not just your parents, but everyone you come into contact with. The end result of resentment and anger is always the same—it consumes the one harboring it more than it affects the person being resented.

Journaling helped me a lot in dealing with anger and resentment. Writing down how I felt about my childhood—without any judgment shed light on some of my experiences and gave me a new perspective. Take responsibility and take care of your inner child every single day, and keep in mind that although it may make you feel better to receive an apology from the people who hurt you. Often, you may not receive that apology. Therefore, being resentful is not the most effective solution to dealing with past trauma. Love heals all wounds—and not just yours, but the wounds of those who have wronged you in the past. Sometimes, loving people may mean loving them from a distance, and that is okay.

What Do I Do When Other People Are In Their Inner Child?

Often, people ask the question, "I am working on healing myself from past trauma, but how do I deal with the people in my life, such as my partner, friends, parents, or employer, when they act out their inner child?" Tensions and conflicts usually escalate when both of you allow your inner child to take over during a confrontation. If you both do not manage your emotions, your conversation will most probably end in an argument.

When you recognize that the person you are talking to is in touch with their inner child, keep the following in mind:

- Recognize that you are probably about to fall into your inner child as well—we tend to go into defensive mode during a confrontation to protect ourselves from a possible threat to our sense of security.

- It is difficult to suddenly shift from your inner child to rational thinking when you have already fallen into defensive mode.
- It is important to take care of your inner child first.
- Communicate that you need some time and space. Try to stay calm and suggest to the other person the appropriate time to continue the conversation.

How To Communicate That You Need Space During A Heated Conversation

Talking to Someone Familiar With Your Healing Process	Talking to Someone Unfamiliar With Your Healing Process
"I can't think clearly right now. I think it's best that I take care of my inner child. Let's talk about this tomorrow morning.	"This conversation is very important but I feel overwhelmed right now. Can we talk about this tomorrow when we are both calmer?"

<table>
<tr><td rowspan="3">“I think we are both emotional right now and this feels like the appropriate time for me to be alone and take care of my inner child. Can we continue this conversation tomorrow?</td><td>“We probably both need some time to cool off. Would you be okay with having this conversation later on?” I think we both need to take a breather.”</td></tr>
<tr><td>“I’d love to continue this conversation but I'm not in the right headspace to talk about this right now. Can we discuss this another time when we can both think clearly?”</td></tr>
<tr><td>“I do appreciate your ideas and opinion on this matter but, I feel a bit overwhelmed right now and need to rest. Would you be okay with talking about this later?</td></tr>
</table>

Giving yourself time and space to reflect on your thoughts, feelings, and emotions is important during your healing process. It allows you to evaluate your reactions and find healthier ways to resolve misunderstandings. After communicating your feelings, it is important to look at what triggered your reaction and practice the exercise outlined in Chapter 6 to help you manage the trigger. Find ways to take care of your inner child and meet his or her needs. This will calm you down and allow you to have a constructive conversation on the suggested date.

What I Do if My Partner Does Not Want to Do Inner Child Healing?

Healing is a personal journey. Your focus should be on you before you try to invite others along on the journey. You cannot force your partner to go on this journey with you; it should be his or her choice to either join you—so that you both work together to help each other heal—or not.

If your partner or family does not want to do the inner child work, it is okay. That does not mean you should love them less. Focus on your journey and do not try to change other people. You can still have a nourishing and healthy relationship with your loved ones even if they are not interested in the inner child healing concept.

When I first started my healing journey, I felt that my partner should do inner child work as well to improve our relationship, and guess what happened? It only caused more problems and harm to the relationship than good. Trying to change others and making them believe in your ideas is often a sign of an unhealed inner child. Conflicts often get out of control when you and your partner act out of your unhealed inner children. Therefore, your goal should be to focus on being calm and taking care of your inner child so you can think level-headedly. If you do inner child work and work even during challenging conflicts, often, you inspire other people to do the same.

How Do I Know That I Am Healing?

When you put in the effort to heal your inner child and meet his or her unmet needs, it is inspiring to see your progress. Often, people wonder how one can tell if they are healing. The first thing is to understand your inner child and how he or she manifests in your behavior. In chapter one, we learned that a wounded inner child usually manifests in the form of:

- low self-esteem
- codependency
- perfectionism
- negative self-image
- self-criticism

When you are familiar with how your inner child manifests itself, it will be easier to see your progress in a specific area of your life. For example, if you are a perfectionist and, in the past, you used to criticize and judge yourself if you believed your performance was not up to standard. When you start healing, you become less judgmental of yourself and more compassionate, and you learn to separate your self-image from your outcomes.

The following signs can help you identify if you are making progress in your healing process.

You Have Regained Your Sense of Curiosity

When you are curious about yourself and your behaviors, you gain a better understanding of your core motivations and why you behave the way you do. This allows you to spot thinking and behavior patterns that repeat themselves. When you understand that these patterns are from your childhood conditioning and are no longer needed, it becomes easier to let go of the negative beliefs that no longer serve you.

You Can Identify Where Your Triggers Stem From

When you become curious about your behavior, it is easy to identify where your triggers stem from. Making the connection between childhood wounds and your triggers can help you find effective ways to meet your inner child's needs.

You Meet Your Inner Child's Needs

Learning to identify your triggers is important in your healing process. It allows you to meet your inner child's needs. When you start healing, you learn to prioritize meeting your needs and become self-reliant, which builds trust between you and your inner child.

You Have Reconnected to Your Playful Side

Making time to play and express your creativity is a sign that you are healing. Playfulness is a sign that you are getting comfortable expressing your authentic self.

You Feel Optimistic and Inspired to Pursue New Activities

When you start healing, you feel confident to pursue new dreams that you would not normally pursue in the past because of fear and a lack of self-confidence. You feel free to pursue new goals, relationships, and passions without the fear of rejection.

You Notice Changes in Your Relationships

Healing your inner child is a personal journey. However, the results can impact your relationships. You learn to manage your emotions, which makes you less reactive and improves your communication skills. When you heal, you become independent instead of codependent, and you become intentional about the types of relationships you build.

You Can Manage Your Emotions

Healing your inner child teaches you how to manage your emotions. When you begin to heal, you learn to acknowledge your emotions. This leads to fewer mood swings and anxiety and allows you to be calmer even in the face of adversity.

You Are Patient and Understand That Healing Is an Ongoing Process

When you start healing, you will become aware that healing is a journey. There will be times when you experience triggers and need to be patient and compassionate with yourself. There will also be times when you need to reach out to people for emotional support. When you focus on your healing journey as a lifelong process, you increase your levels of patience and self-acceptance.

As you embark on your healing journey, keep the following ideas in mind:

- Healing is a lifelong process; be patient with yourself and focus on the process instead of the results.
- A wounded inner child affects all areas of your life—your relationships, career, finances, and your self-image.
- It is important to identify how your inner child manifests themself in each area of your life.
- Learn to assess the core beliefs that impact each area of your life. This will help you let go of beliefs that no longer serve you.

- It is normal to feel anger toward the people who have caused you pain in the past. However, staying angry forever is not an effective solution to healing past wounds.
- Throughout your healing process, you will encounter other people—some of whom are experiencing their own inner child. It is important to meet your inner child's needs in order to find effective ways to manage your emotions when you encounter someone in their own inner child.
- Remember, you cannot force your family or partner to practice inner child healing with you. It should be their decision if they want to practice the concept to support you on your healing journey.
- To help you track your healing progress identify the following:
    - Have you regained your sense of curiosity?
    - Are you able to recognize your triggers and where they stem from?
    - Do you meet your inner child's needs?
    - Do you make time to play and express your creative side?

- Do you feel optimistic and inspired to pursue new activities?
- Are your relationships more positive than before?
- Are you calmer and have learned to manage your emotions?

I hope that I have managed to answer some of the questions you may have about inner healing not just in this chapter but throughout this book. Curiosity is the best teacher. The more we ask questions about certain aspects of our lives the more we open ourselves to learning.

Conclusion

As soon as healing takes place, go out and heal somebody else. –Serina Hartwell

I hope that this book has inspired you to take action and begin your healing journey. Perhaps you are unclear about where to start or what steps to take now that you have the tools and practices to heal your inner child. You may be wondering what you should do if you find yourself slipping back into your old behavior and thinking patterns, or whether or not the exercises outlined in this book will work for you. First, let me say, breathe. When your mind starts racing with these questions, take a deep breath and remember that healing is a process that requires time and patience.

Where should you begin your healing journey? The first step in any healing process is to acknowledge that you need healing. If you cannot accept that you have emotional issues that you need to work on, it will be difficult to start the healing process. Acknowledging that your inner child exists is an important step toward reconnecting with him or her.

Perhaps another question you may have is, "I've reconnected with my inner child; what now? Do I continue doing the exercises?" Remember the story I shared at the beginning of this book about the first time I practiced inner child healing? Back then, I was recovering from an eating disorder. I had quite a lot of unresolved emotional issues, and I was unhappy with my body. The root cause of my emotional issues was not my physical appearance but had to do with the beliefs I had about myself. Inner child healing helped me overcome my eating disorder, but when I began to feel better about myself, I stopped practicing the concept. However, I later discovered that I still had wounds that needed to be healed in other areas of my life. You see, it is not enough to read this book and practice the exercises outlined in it a few times. You have to consistently apply the ideas and exercises I have shared throughout this book to achieve positive results. Healing is a lifelong process that requires patience and consistency.

Inner child healing is the process of reparenting yourself. It is giving your inner child all the things he or she never had in your childhood, such as love, affection, acceptance, validation, and protection. Reconnecting with your inner child means building and nurturing your relationship with him or her. You have to show up for your inner child every day, like a good parent would for the child they love. Understanding this will help you in times when you feel like giving up.

"What if I fall back into my old behavior and thinking patterns after practicing inner child healing?" you may wonder. Every child that learns to walk falls from time to time. Sometimes they bruise their tiny knees and elbows, but that does not stop them from continuing to learn how to walk. Children always find the inspiration to get up and keep moving forward—despite the challenges they face. There is a lesson here for all of us. When you find yourself falling into your old patterns, try not to beat yourself up. Instead, look for ways that inspire you to stick to your healing process. Spend time doing the things that connect you to your inner child. In chapter seven, we learned different ways to reconnect with your inner child. You can try creating more playtime and doing activities your inner child loves. It could be watching your favorite movie, spending time in nature, or reading your favorite book. Or, you can try something creative like painting or cooking your favorite meal. Incorporating the exercises outlined in this book into your daily routine can also help reduce the chances of falling back into old patterns. For example, practicing self-care and self-love every day allows you to put your inner child's needs first. When your inner child's needs are met, you feel happier, calmer, safer, and more optimistic.

If, at any point during your healing process, you feel overwhelmed, remember that you do not have to do the work alone. Consider seeking the help of a counselor. Speaking to a therapist can help you find healthy ways to deal with emotional trauma. I have included a meditation practice in Chapter 7 to help you reconnect with your inner child. Meditation is an effective tool to help clear mental noise when you cannot silence negative thoughts. Practicing meditation every day can help you feel grounded and connected.

As you go through your healing process, keep this in mind; the goal of inner child healing is to meet your inner child's unmet needs. Practice self-compassion and self-love, learn to validate your feelings and emotions, set healthy boundaries in your life, let go of old, negative beliefs, and open yourself to learning new beliefs that align with who you truly are. This will help you learn to express yourself without fear of judgment and allow you to be your authentic self.

Finally, I just want to say that I admire your courage and willingness to embark on this journey. Healing takes courage, and not everyone finds the courage to face their past wounds. Your determination to find solutions to help you overcome emotional trauma is proof enough that hope exists in all of us. I hope that as you practice inner child healing and the exercises I have outlined in this book, you will find healing and embrace your true essence. I hope this journey of self-discovery will be as beautiful and fulfilling for you as it has been for me, and that as you find healing, you will encourage healing in those around you as well. As Mark Nepo once said, "When we heal ourselves, we heal the world. For as the body is only as healthy as its individual cells, the world is only as healthy as its individual souls" (Book of Awakening, n.d.).

Thank you

I would like to personally thank you for purchasing this book and giving me the opportunity to be a part of your journey.

You had a wide choice of books, but you chose this one, and you made it all the way to the end of the book!

So, a big THANK YOU.

One last thing before you go, may I ask you to leave a review or rating if the information within this book helped you. This is the best way to support my work and help me continue publishing new books.

Your support means a lot to me.

Thank you

Reference

7 Inner Child Archetypes. (2021, August 6). Wysteria Edwards. www.wysteriaedwards.com/blog/7%20Inner%20Child%20Archetypes

A quote by David Richo. (n.d.). Goodreads. Retrieved March 19, 2023, from www.goodreads.com/quotes/372660-our-wounds-are-often-the-openings-into-the-best-and

A quote by Erik Pevernagie. (n.d.). Goodreads. Retrieved March 17, 2023, from www.goodreads.com/quotes/10218976-let-us-listen-to-the-needs-of-our-inner-child

A quote by Maya Angelou. (n.d.). Goodreads. Retrieved March 20, 2023, from www.goodreads.com/quotes/493926-as-soon-as-healing-takes-place-go-out-and-heal

A quote by Serina Hartwell. (n.d.). Goodreads. Retrieved March 20, 2023, from www.goodreads.com/quotes/1353935-we-nurture-our-creativity-when-we-release-our-inner-child

A quote from Joe Jones. (n.d.). Goodreads. Retrieved March 8, 2023, from www.goodreads.com/quotes/271557-after-a-while-the-middle-aged-person-who-lives-in-her

A quote from Soul Works - The Minds Journal Collection. (n.d.). Goodreads. Retrieved March 1, 2023, from www.goodreads.com/quotes/11190042-inside-of-each-of-us-is-just-an-inner-child

A quote from The Book of Awakening. (n.d.). Goodreads. Retrieved March 25, 2023, from www.goodreads.com/quotes/9093394-when-we-heal-ourselves-we-heal-the-world-for-as#:~:text=Quote%20by%20Mark%20Nepo%3A%20%E2%80%9CWhen

A. A. Milne Quote. (n.d.). A-Z Quotes. Retrieved February 27, 2023, from www.azquotes.com/quote/664517

Adey, O. (2022, January 31). *2022 - Psychology: According to expert, there are 7 archetypes of the inner child - which one are you?* Get to Next. gettotext.com/psychology-according-to-expert-there-are-7-archetypes-of-the-inner-child-which-one-are-you/

Aldana, R. (2015, December 6). *5 Common Emotional Wounds from Childhood.* Step to Health. steptohealth.com/emotional-wounds-childhood/

All I hear is the symphony Quotes by Silvery Afternoon. (n.d.). Goodreads. Retrieved March 4, 2023, from www.goodreads.com/work/quotes/95973141-all-i-hear-is-the-symphony

Bank Lees, A. (2020, October 28). *7 Tools for Managing Traumatic Stress* |. NAMI: National Alliance on Mental Illness. www.nami.org/Blogs/NAMI-Blog/October-2020/7-Tools-for-Managing-Traumatic-Stress

Brodeur, M. (n.d.). *10 Negative Body Image Thoughts You Need to Stop Right Now.* Verily. Retrieved March 22, 2023, from verilymag.com/2016/12/negative-body-image-mental-health

Campbell, E. (2015). *Six Surprising Benefits of Curiosity.* Greater Good. greatergood.berkeley.edu/article/item/six_surprising_benefits_of_curiosity

Chauhan, S. (2020, December 20). *Who Is Your Inner Child | Highbrow.* Gohighbrow. gohighbrow.com/who-is-your-inner-child/

Choix, J. (n.d.). *How To Improve Your Relationships By Healing Your Inner Child Wounds.* Mywellbeing. Retrieved March 3, 2023, from https://mywellbeing.com/ask-a-therapist/improve-your-relationships#:~:text=The%20inner%20child%20in%20us

Cooks-Campbell, A. (2022a, March 15). *How Inner Child Work Enables Healing and Playful Discovery.* Better Up. www.betterup.com/blog/inner-child-work

Cooks-Campbell, A. (2022b, July 15). *Triggers: Learn to Recognize and Deal With Them.* Betterup. www.betterup.com/blog/triggers

Creativity and Personal Development. (2020, February 25). Exploring Your Mind. exploringyourmind.com/creativity-and-personal-development/

Divorce Rate in America: 48 Divorce Statistics. (2023, January 3). Divorce.com. divorce.com/blog/divorce-statistics/

Dr. Bruce Lipton Explains How Your Childhood May Have Messed You Up. (2019, July 1).

Capitalist Creations. capitalistcreations.com/youve-got-some-looming-childhood-issues/

Engelke, M. (2017, February 26). *7 common negative beliefs and the problems they cause • Liberty Counselling Luxembourg*. Liberty Counselling Luxembourg. libertycounsellingluxembourg.com/7-common-negative-beliefs-and-the-problems-they-cause/

Estrada, J. (2022, December 10). *How Healed Is Your Inner Child? These Are 8 Strong Signs*. Well+Good. www.wellandgood.com/signs-youre-healing-your-inner-child/

5 Emotional Wounds During Childhood That Last Into Adulthood. (2018, September 4). You Are Mom. youaremom.com/children/emotional-wounds-during-childhood/

Hailey, L. (2022, April 15). *How to Set Boundaries: 5 Ways to Draw the Line Politely*. Science of People. www.scienceofpeople.com/how-to-set-boundaries/

Happy. (2022, April 6). *Injustice Trauma: Signs and Tips to Heal*. Psych Crumbs. psychcrumbs.com/injustice-trauma/#:~:text=What%20Does%20Injustice%20Trauma%20Mean

Hartney, E. (2022, November 22). *How Emotional Pain Addiction Causes Physical Issues*. Verywell Mind. www.verywellmind.com/physical-pain-and-emotional-pain-22421

Healing the inner child through affirmation. (2020, November 4). Australian Centre for Meditation and Mindfulness. www.meditationandmindfulness.com.au/blog/healing-the-inner-child-through-affirmation/

Holland, K. (2019, November 25). *Childhood Emotional Neglect: What It Is, and How It Can Affect You*. Healthline. www.healthline.com/health/mental-health/childhood-emotional-neglect#effects-in-adulthood

How to Cope with Childhood Trauma Triggers. (n.d.). Stonewater Recovery. Retrieved March 18, 2023, from www.stonewaterrecovery.com/adolescent-treatment-blog/how-to-cope-with-childhood-trauma-triggers

How to heal your inner child - My Therapy Assistant. (2021, October 13). My Therapy Assistant. www.mytherapyassistant.com/blog/do-you-have-a-wounded-inner-child-here-are-7-key-signs

How to Heal Your Painful Memories, Thoughts, & Beliefs to Create a Greater Future with Dr. Nicole LePera. (2021, March 12). Lewis Howes. lewishowes.com/podcast/how-to-heal-your-painful-memories-thoughts-beliefs-to-create-a-greater-future-with-dr-nicole-lepera/

How To Recognize If Your Childhood Trauma Is Affecting You As An Adult (& How To Heal). (2019, October 1). Michigan ACE Initiative. www.miace.org/2019/10/01/how-to-recognize-if-your-childhood-trauma-is-affecting-you-as-an-adult-how-to-heal/

Inner-Child Work: Overview, Benefits, and Effectiveness. (2019, October 19). The Human Condition. thehumancondition.com/inner-child-work-benefits-effectiveness/

Is Your Inner Child Ruining Your Adult Life? | ReGain. (2023, February 14). Regain Us.

www.regain.us/advice/general/is-your-inner-child-ruining-your-adult-life/

July 21, E. Y., & 2021. (2023, March 1). *This Is What It Looks Like to Set Personal and Emotional Boundaries.* Real Simple. www.realsimple.com/health/mind-mood/emotional-health/how-to-set-boundaries

Kinsey, M. (2022, October 19). *What Are Attachment Styles & How Do They Influence Adult Behavior?* Choosing Therapy. www.choosingtherapy.com/attachment-styles/

Kristenson, S. (2022, October 25). *How to Heal Your Inner Child: A 7-Step Guide.* Happier Human. www.happierhuman.com/heal-inner-child/

LeBlanc, M. (2022, July 11). *The Power of Your Inner Child and the Process of Reparenting.* Chopra. chopra.com/articles/the-power-of-your-inner-child-and-the-process-of-reparenting#:~:text=Reparenting%20is%20when%20we%20come

Lepera, N. (2021). *How to Do the Work : Recognize Your Patterns, Heal from Your Past, and*

Create Your Self. Harpercollins Publishers. (Original work published 1 B.C.E.)

Lipton, B. H. (2016). *The biology of belief : unleashing the power of consciousness, matter & miracles* (p. 172). Hay House, Inc. (Original work published 2005)

Lorraine Dawn Nilon. (2017). *Your Insight and Awareness Book.* Lorraine Nilon. (Original work published 2023)

Luna, A. (2019, April 6). *25 Signs You Have a Wounded Inner Child (and How to Heal) ⋆ LonerWolf.*LonerWolf. lonerwolf.com/feeling-safe-inner-child/

Mantilla, S. (2022, February 7). *19 Toxic Limiting Beliefs About Money and How To Overcome Them.* Money Tamer. moneytamer.com/limiting-beliefs-about-money/

Martin, S. (2020, April 23). *7 Types of Boundaries You May Need.* Psych Central. psychcentral.com/blog/imperfect/2020/04 /7-types-of-boundaries-you-may-need#7)-Non-Negotiable-Boundaries

Miranda, L. (n.d.). *6 Steps to Breaking Your Limiting Beliefs*. PushFar. Retrieved March

17, 2023, from www.pushfar.com/article/6-steps-to-breaking-your-limiting-beliefs/

Pattemore, C. (2021, June 3). *10 Ways to Build and Preserve Better Boundaries*. Psych Central. psychcentral.com/lib/10-way-to-build-and-preserve-better-boundaries

Publishing, W. (2017, June 26). *Writing a Letter to Your Inner Child*. Mental Movement Magazine. www.mentalmovement.co.uk/writing-a-letter-to-your-inner-child/

Ray, A. (2012). *Nonviolence : the transforming power* (p. 30). Inner Light Publishers. (Original work published 2023)

Raypole, C. (2020, June 26). *Inner Child: 6 Ways to Find Yours*. Healthline. www.healthline.com/health/inner-child

Raypole, C. (2021, September 9). *8 Tips for Healing Your Inner Child*. Healthline. www.healthline.com/health/mental-health/inner-child-healing#acknowledge

Roncero, A. (2022, October 22). *The Unspoken Truth about Trauma: How It Truly Affects Your Life*. Www.betterup.com. www.betterup.com/blog/trauma

7 Inner Child Archetypes. (2021, August 6). Wysteria Edwards. www.wysteriaedwards.com/blog/7%20Inner%20Child%20Archetypes

Stephens, C. (2016, August 30). *10 Career Beliefs You Should Stop Right Now*. LinkedIn. www.linkedin.com/pulse/10-career-beliefs-you-should-stop-right-now-craig-stephens

Stuck? How Your Inner Child Can Help. (2022, August 5). Randytaran.com. www.randytaran.com/blog/stuck-how-your-inner-child-can-help

Sweet, J. (2014, May 25). *7 Negative Thoughts That Prevent a Happy Life & Career*. Wishingwell Coaching with Jessica Sweet. wishingwellcoach.com/negative-thoughts-life-career/

The Power of Tattoos Quotes by Cary G. Weldy. (n.d.). Goodreads. Retrieved March 13, 2023, from www.goodreads.com/work/quotes/86732504-the-power-of-tattoos-twelve-hidden-energy-secrets-of-body-art-every-tat#:~:text=%E2%80%9CHealing%20journeys%20do%20not%20necessarily

The Ten Secrets of Montessori - #3 The Absorbent Mind. (n.d.). Aimmontessoriteachertraining.org. Retrieved March 7, 2023, from aimmontessoriteachertraining.org/the-ten-secrets-of-montessori-education-3-the-absorbent-mind/

Turonova, S. (2023). *How to Love Yourself After Surviving Childhood Trauma*. Silvia Turon. silviaturon.com/how-to-love-yourself-after-surviving-childhood-trauma/

Understanding Trauma Triggers and How to Manage Them. (2021, December 16). The Dawn. thedawnrehab.com/blog/understanding-trauma-triggers-and-how-to-manage-them/

Walters, O. & M. (2021, January 21). *25 Limiting Beliefs That Interfere With Finding True Love (Plus How To Turn Them Around)*. Love on Purpose. www.loveonpurpose.com/25-limiting-beliefs-that-interfere-with-finding-true-love/

Webb, J. (2018, September 30). *The 2 Types Of Childhood Emotional Neglect: Active and Passive*. Psych Central. psychcentral.com/blog/childhood-neglect/2018/09/the-2-types-of-childhood-emotional-neglect-active-and-passive#1

Williamson, J. (2020, June 16). *An Open Letter to My Inner Child*. Healing Brave. healingbrave.com/blogs/all/open-letter-to-my-inner-child

Wright, S. A. (2021, November 8). *Trauma Triggers: How to Identify and Overcome Triggers*. Psych Central. https://psychcentral.com/health/trauma-triggers#what-are-triggers

Your Insight and Awareness Book Quotes by Lorraine Nilon. (n.d.). Goodreads. Retrieved February 26, 2023, from www.goodreads.com/work/quotes/58241932-your-insight-and-awareness-book-your-life-is-an-expedition-to-discover

Zaayer Kaufman, C. (2011). *Here are six common career-limiting beliefs and how you can reframe them in a more constructive light*. Monster Career Advice. www.monster.com/career-advice/article/career-limiting-beliefs

Made in the USA
Middletown, DE
09 May 2023